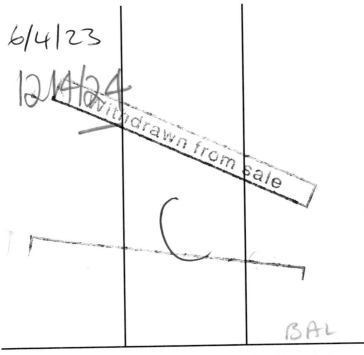

6/4/23

12/4/24

Withdrawn from sale

BAL

Please renew or return items by the date shown on your receipt

www.hertfordshire.gov.uk/libraries

Renewals and enquiries: 0300 123 4049

Textphone for hearing or 0300 123 4041
speech impaired users:

L32 11.16

OTHER TITLES IN THE COMPACT GUIDE SERIES

Winston Churchill

The Cold War

DNA

The Elements

Queen Elizabeth II

THIS IS AN ANDRE DEUTSCH BOOK

Text © Richard Holmes 2005
Design © Andre Deutsch 2019

Originally published in 2005 under the title *The Napoleonic Wars Experience*.
This edition published in 2019 by Andre Deutsch
A division of the Carlton Publishing Group
20 Mortimer Street
London
W1T 3JW

Typeset by JCS Publishing Services Ltd

Printed in Italy
A CIP catalogue for this book is available from the British Library

ISBN: 978-0-233-00594-2

CONTENTS

THE AGE OF NAPOLEON

**Few periods of history are more resonantly
defined by the name of one man.**

Napoleon bestrode early nineteenth-century Europe like the proverbial colossus. By 1812, most of the continent was under his control: his writ ran from southern Spain to the Baltic and from the Atlantic to Russia. He had defeated all but one of the great powers, and save for Britain's "moat defensive", it is hard to see how the country could have been spared. He had installed family members on half a dozen thrones, dictated terms to the heads of ancient dynasties, and married the Holy Roman Emperor's daughter. He had recast his country's administrative, educational and legal systems, stabilized its currency and set up the Bank of France, created a new aristocracy and instituted the Légion d'Honneur. He was a patron of the arts, and filled French museums with the spoils of his conquests. He was the towering figure of his age, and foresaw that his achievements would make it impossible for even opponents to ignore him: "It will be difficult to make me disappear from the public memory. French historians will have to deal with the Empire and will have to give me my rightful due."

But what is his rightful due? As we look back at Napoleon, it is difficult not to be both attracted and repelled, and in my own lifetime I have rarely been able to strike a balanced view. My mother took me to Paris when I was 10 years old, and the sight of Napoleon's tomb shining coldly beneath the dome of Les Invalides stirred my emotions in a way that I still remember today. When I was researching for my doctorate in the archives at Vincennes, I was within musket-shot of the ditch where the Duc d'Enghien, kidnapped from neutral Baden, was shot by firing squad in 1804, the victim of judicial murder: my former idol had blood on his hands.

On a dozen battlefields from Austerlitz to Wagram I have seen a man who could defeat huge armies, as he did at Austerlitz; pulverize the military giant of its day, as he did at Jena; and dart between larger opponents, lunging at each in turn, as he did in France in 1814. He could inspire the fiercest loyalty. When Napoleon was hit in the ankle at Ratisbon in 1809, there was a rumour that he was badly wounded, and men flocked in from all directions. Light cavalry officer Marcellin Marbot saw how: "In a moment thousands of men surrounded Napoleon, in spite of enemy cannon fire which concentrated on this huge group." In 1803, young Charles Parquin, a trooper in the *Chasseurs à Cheval*, was a sentry outside Napoleon's quarters: "I still recall with what joy and pride I did sentry duty outside the apartment he was occupying ... I do not think I have ever known a finer experience than my sentry duty outside the door of a man on whom the eyes of all Europe were already fixed." A young officer, mortally wounded before taking a message to Napoleon, braced up for his last duty. "You're wounded," said the Emperor. "No, Sire, killed," said the youngster proudly. When General Levesque de la Ferrière was having his leg amputated in 1814, during the operation, which he bore with great courage, the general repeatedly called out: "Long live the Emperor!"

French Military Ranks

The army of the old regime and the restored Bourbons had only two grades of general officer, *maréchal de camp* (equivalent to brigadier) and *lieutenant-général*. The revolutionaries replaced these with *général de brigade* and *général de division* respectively. The appointment of marshal – Marshal of France under the Bourbons and Marshal of the Empire under Napoleon – was a dignity of state rather than simply a military rank. There are a number of semantic traps. For instance, a *brigadier* was (and remains) a corporal in the cavalry or artillery, and a *maréchal des logis* a sergeant in the same arms; a colonel, under the Revolution, was styled *chef de brigade*; and *major-général* referred to the appointment of chief of staff rather than a rank. Berthier, though a marshal, habitually signed himself as *major-général*, and referring to a *général de brigade* as *"brigadier"* remains a sure way of losing friends. In these pages I translate *général de brigade* as brigadier and *général de division* as general of division.

Yet Napoleon could inspire such behaviour with utter cynicism. He said that a man would not sell his life but would give it away for a piece of ribbon. If he was merciless to Enghien, he could be brutal on a far larger scale: in 1799 he ordered his men to kill perhaps 2,000 Turkish prisoners, some of whom were bayonetted to save ammunition. He was a consummate liar. When a secretary, penning a characteristically mendacious dispatch for him, acknowledged that "I had found it painful recording these official words at his dictation," Napoleon retorted, "You are a simpleton. You really don't understand a thing." He could be callous, telling his wife Josephine that he was divorcing her because she could not conceive: "Madam, I need a womb." He could not distinguish the interests of France from his own, leading one historian, who suggested that three million men were killed in his wars, to claim that "the memory of Genghis Khan paled in comparison". So there is no simple view to take: a figure of Napoleon's extraordinary stature both dazzles and burns.

Richard Holmes

THE REVOLUTIONARY CALENDAR

Between 24 October 1793 and 1 January 1806 France used a revolutionary calendar intended to emphasize her radical break with the past, jettison religious and historical baggage, and incorporate both mathematical logic and a regard for nature. After lengthy discussions involving the agronomist Romme, the mathematician Monge, the poets Chénier and Fabre d'Eglantine and the painter David, the calendar came into use in 1793, though it was reckoned from 22 September 1792, the day the Republic came into being, which became 1st Vendémiaire Year I. Year I incorporated 1792–93, Year II 1793–94, and Year XIV, the last of the system, 1805–06.

There were 12 months, and all had names based on nature and rhyming three by three to reflect the "sonority" of the seasons. Autumn had Vendémiaire (vintage), Brumaire (misty) and Frimaire (frosty); winter comprised Nivôse (snowy), Pluiviôse (rainy) and Ventôse (windy); spring enjoyed Germinal (seeding), Floréal (flowering) and Prairial (meadowy); and summer had Messidor (harvest), Thermidor (hot) and Fructidor (fruiting).

A month had 30 days, divided into three *décades* of ten days apiece, named from *primidi* for the first to *décadi* for the tenth day. As this meant that there was now one non-working day in ten, rather than one in seven, there was not a little grumbling. Saint's days had been abolished, and each day now had a name connected with flora, fauna or honest toil: 23 Vendémiaire, for instance, was named for the turnip, 4 Ventôse for the billy goat and 20 Prarial for the pitchfork. Each day was divided into ten hours, each hour into 100 minutes and each minute into 100 seconds. As this made all existing clocks obsolete it was far from popular and generally disappeared in 1795. Five extra days (six in leap years) at the end of each year were national holidays. As New Year's Day was meant to fall on the autumnal equinox, whose date could not be easily predicted, there were to be leap years. The system was abolished by Napoleon but briefly revived by the Paris Communards in 1871 – Year LXXIX.

CHAPTER ONE

THE

REVOLUTIONARY

BACKGROUND

But for the French Revolution, Napoleone di Buonaparte, who until 1796 customarily spelled his name in the Italian fashion, might never have come to history's notice, remaining just an obscure artillery officer.

However, when a blast of radical change blew away most of those in authority, from King Louis XVI himself to many junior officers and minor officials, it swept in new men, several of whom speedily fell victim to a monster which devoured its own children. For the agile and ambitious this was a time of extraordinary opportunity – as well as great danger.

The Revolution's proximate cause was the summoning of the Estates-General – a national assembly with medieval antecedents – representing the nobility, the clergy and the Third Estate (all those belonging to neither of the two preceding classes) to discuss finances. These had been ruined by the American War of Independence, in which France played a decisive part in helping Britain's colonies throw off their yoke. Deeper causes included resistance to absolute monarchy amongst the largely tax-exempt privileged classes. Royal authority was weakened by the growing revolt of the Estates-General, and, as Maximilien Robespierre, who became a leader of the extremists, admitted, "the people appeared on the scene only later".

They were encouraged to do so because a bad harvest in 1788 followed a period of economic deterioration characterized by high unemployment. Food shortages were exacerbated by rumours that monopolists were causing scarcity for their own ends. The Third Estate constructed its programme based on *cahiers* – lists of grievances – which testified, amongst other things, to the desire of the urban middle class to gain equality with the more privileged, and for the peasants to escape obligations rooted in the feudal past. The Estates-General met on 5 May 1789, and on 17 June, the Third Estate, exasperated by the ruling that the Estates should sit and vote separately, declared itself the National Assembly, and a number of noblemen and clergy joined it. In an atmosphere full of wild rumours, the crowds that thronged the capital sought arms to defend themselves against a military coup. Early on 14 July, they found some at Les Invalides, and moved on to the Bastille, a fortress and state prison on the eastern edge of Paris, which surrendered after a brief defence.

Three days later, Louis went to the Hôtel de Ville to receive the new national cockade of red, white and blue, but on 6 October a mob invaded the king's palace at Versailles and took him back to Paris. The Declaration of Rights, passed by the Assembly on 26 August, had affirmed that men were free and equal, and that sovereignty resided in the people. Church lands were sold off and paper money was issued, and the Constituent Assembly discussed wholesale reform. As old institutions were swept away, real power resided in political clubs like the Jacobins and the

Maximilien Robespierre (1758–1794)

Robespierre, a lawyer from Arras, was elected to the Estates-General
in 1789. His rhetoric and vaunted incorruptibility gave him enormous
influence, not only in the Convention but also with the Paris mob, and,
having disposed of his rivals (including Danton), by the early summer
of 1794 he was the most powerful man in France. In July, however, the
Convention, horrified by the flood of executions, turned against him.
He was arrested on 27 July, with his jaw smashed by a bullet, probably
in a suicide attempt, and was guillotined the following day.

Cordeliers. In June 1791, the king and queen failed in an escape attempt
and although Louis signed a new monarchical constitution, things were
spiralling out of control.

In August 1791, Austria and Prussia affirmed their readiness to help
Louis. Meanwhile, France itself became increasingly bellicose, declaring
war on Austria and Prussia in April of the following year. Early French
reverses and counter-revolutionary movements in the provinces
encouraged the growth of extremism, and in August 1792, the Paris
mob stormed the Tuileries. A National Convention, elected by universal
suffrage, replaced the Legislative Assembly. This new body declared
France a republic, but in early September the mob massacred hundreds
of prisoners, showing how unstable things had become. In January 1793,
Louis was executed for treason, and the next month the Convention
went on to declare war on Britain and Holland.

The new executive, the Committee of Public Safety, was supported
by a Convention purged of moderates and dominated by the left-wing
majority called "the Mountain". In a spasm of terror, the guillotine
claimed the lives of Queen Marie-Antoinette, counter-revolutionaries,
unsuccessful generals and revolutionaries alike. The revolutionary
Camille Desmoulins quipped that the gods were thirsty, but himself
died in the spring of 1794 when members of two rival factions were
guillotined. From 10 June to 27 July, some 1,376 prisoners were executed in Paris, dismaying politicians who feared that they, too, would
be engulfed: on 28–29 July (10–11 Thermidor in the new revolutionary

Louis XVI (1754–1793)

Louis XVI was third son of the Dauphin, eldest son of Louis XV: his father and elder brothers all died before him. When he came to the throne in 1774, France was in serious financial difficulties, and her involvement in the War of American Independence worsened them. Louis was initially popular, though his Austrian-born wife Marie-Antoinette was not, but he proved unable to steer a steady course between reform and reaction. After apparently supporting the Revolution, he tried to flee France, and was guillotined on 21 January 1793.

calendar) Robespierre and his Jacobin adherents, authors of the worst extremism, were themselves executed. This "thermidorian reaction" was consolidated when the army supported the Convention against the mob in May 1795, and a new constitution was ratified by plebiscite. On 5 October (13 Vendémiaire), the mob again assailed the Convention but was dispersed by troops. The cannon whose "whiff of grapeshot" winnowed the rioters were commanded, as we shall soon see, by a young brigadier-general called Napoleon Bonaparte. A new executive, the Directory, now worked with a moderate Convention to bring the first stability France had enjoyed for six years.

CHAPTER TWO

THE MAKING

OF A

REPUTATION

**On 15 August 1769, Letizia Buonaparte
was hurried to her home in the Corsican
capital, Ajaccio, to give birth to a boy, who
was christened Napoleone.**

His father, Carlo Maria (who now called himself Charles), was a lawyer who had supported Paoli's Corsican nationalists, but after their defeat by the French earlier the same year, had got on well with the authorities and served as a municipal councillor. He capitalized on his status in the minor nobility to secure support for his burgeoning family, and in 1779 Napoleon – for such we will now call him – entered the Royal School at Brienne (in Champagne) with a scholarship.

The boy was unhappy: his small stature and appalling French encouraged bullying, but he would not be coerced. When a master sought to make him eat on his knees, he riposted: "In my family we kneel only before God!" His reports were mixed. Most testified to academic success, especially in mathematics, but also to an "imperious and stubborn" character. In October 1784, aged 15, he moved to the *École Militaire* in Paris. Hopeless at drill and German, he again excelled at mathematics, though when he was commissioned into the artillery in 1785, he ranked forty-second out of 56 students.

Stationed at Valence, Napoleon spent much of his time in private study. In 1787, he enjoyed a long leave, trying to sort out family affairs – for his father had died – and did not return to his regiment, now at Auxonne, until June 1788. Here, he was influenced by the talented commandant of the artillery school, Baron du Teil, who not only developed Napoleon's skills in gunnery, but helped lay the foundations of the tactical concepts which he would later develop to such outstanding effect. However, he was dismally short of money, and in 1788 endured a long illness.

Paul Barras (1755–1829)

Barras, a count and former infantry officer, became a member of the Jacobin club and in 1793 voted in the Convention for the king's execution. Instrumental in the fall of Robespierre, he went on to act firmly against royalists and Jacobins alike, and in 1795 summoned Bonaparte to deal with the mob. He was a member of the Directory, but his sybaritic ways (amongst his mistresses was Napoleon's future wife Josephine) made him unpopular, and he was easily ousted in the Brumaire coup of November 1799.

In August 1789, Napoleon took six months' leave, and once back in Corsica he threw himself into the revolutionary torrent, first asking the National Assembly for aid against the royalist authorities and then trying to attract the support of Paoli, who headed the island's new government. Early in 1791, he returned to regimental duty at Auxonne, but took advantage of an instruction which authorized officers to seek election to newly raised volunteer battalions without forfeiting regular commissions.

On 1 April 1792, Napoleon was elected Lieutenant-Colonel in the Ajaccio volunteers, but helped suppress riots too vigorously, and earned the displeasure of Paoli. He then heard that his regiment in France had ordered a snap muster of all officers, and had struck his name from its rolls. Napoleon rushed to Paris, where he witnessed the storming of the Tuileries, and returned confirmed as a regular captain and volunteer lieutenant-colonel.

Napoleon's baptism of fire occurred in Sardinia where, in early 1793, an expedition from Corsica was ignominiously repulsed. Worse, it was clear that he was now unwelcome in Corsica, and in June 1793 he moved his family to France and resumed his duties there. While he was collecting a gunpowder convoy, a royalist revolt broke out in the Midi, and Napoleon helped suppress it. Unrest spread to Toulon, which admitted an Anglo-Spanish fleet. Napoleon replaced General Carteaux's wounded artillery commander, and his fierce energy and consummate professional skill made him the hero of a siege which ended victoriously on 19 December. He was made temporary Brigadier-General three days later, and confirmed in the rank in February 1794.

Appointed to command the artillery in the Army of Italy, Napoleon, friend of Robespierre's brother and author of a Jacobin-inspired play, was imprisoned in August after the thermidorian reaction. Released two weeks later, he helped ensure a satisfactory end to the year's campaigning in Italy, but, exasperated at being shunted off to an insignificant command, resigned. Military reversals led to his rapid reinstatement, but he was again removed from the army, and Napoleon was technically a civilian when Paul Barras, a member of the Directory, summoned him on 13 Vendémiaire (5 October 1795) to protect the Convention against insurrection. Napoleon opened fire on the Paris mob with artillery, his "whiff of grapeshot" effectively ending the revolt. His action that day was decisive: by its end his political support matched his military reputation.

A R T I L L E R Y

A gunner by training, Napoleon affirmed that "great battles are won by artillery", and paid particular attention to its use, especially that of his "belles filles", the 12-pounders which he sought to mass against the crucial point of his opponent's position.

The artillery Napoleon inherited had suffered less than other arms from the purges and emigrations which accompanied the Revolution. In the 1760s and 1770s, French artillery had been reorganized according to the system devised by Jean-Baptiste Vaquette de Gribeauval, with standardized 4-, 8- and 12-pounders, 6-inch howitzers, carriages, ammunition wagons and tools. Gribeauval introduced elevating screws instead of wedges, and accurately made barrels and ammunition, which ensured that shot fitted snugly, enabling propellant charges (and thus barrel weights) to be reduced without loss of range. Siege artillery was heavier, for its balls had to penetrate the squat ramparts that then characterized fortification. Mortars, whose explosive projectiles were fired at a high angle, were primarily used in sieges.

The 4-pounders were "regimental" pieces, assigned to the infantry, and in 1804–05, as part of a change of equipment to the "System of the Year XIII", Napoleon replaced them with captured 6-pounders. These proved too heavy, and led to the brief abandonment of regimental artillery. It was reintroduced in 1809, but all the regimental pieces were then lost on the retreat from Moscow and were not replaced. The same Year XIII reforms increased the proportion of 12-pounders, and brought a 24-pounder howitzer into service. By 1813, Napoleon sought to have a ratio of five guns of all types for every 1,000 men in his army, but this was never achieved.

Jean-Baptiste Vaquette de Gribeauval (1715–1789)

Gribeauval joined the artillery in 1732 and gained valuable experience while attached to the Austrian army during the Seven Years' War. In 1765, he began his work on the reorganization of the French artillery, and became Inspector-General of the arm in 1776. He was responsible for improving pay, conditions and training, and bequeathed the army of the Revolution and Empire some outstanding gunner officers, amongst them Napoleon Bonaparte.

Gun detachments varied from the eight trained gunners and seven assistants serving the 12-pounder to six and four men respectively for the 4-pounder. A gun was loaded by having its barrel swabbed to extinguish smouldering residue from the previous charge. A cartridge, black powder contained in fabric, was inserted into the muzzle and rammed home, and a projectile followed. Often cartridge and projectile were united to form "fixed ammunition". One of the detachment poked a pricker into the touch-hole to pierce the cartridge, and inserted a firing tube of fine gunpowder. The weapon was aimed, and was fired by having a portfire – a length of smouldering quick-match on a short staff – applied to its touch-hole. The recoil hurled the gun backwards, and the detachment, using handspikes and ropes, hauled it back into position before the process recommenced. A 12-pounder might get off one round a minute, with lighter pieces managing two or three.

Alexandre Antoine Hureau de Sénarmont (1769–1810)

Commissioned in 1785, Sénarmont threw in his lot with the Revolution. He hauled his guns across the Alps in 1800 and handled them well at Marengo. But he made his reputation as a brigadier at Friedland in 1807, where, commanding the artillery of Victor's corps, he moved his guns ever closer to the Russian infantry and hit perhaps 4,000 men in 25 minutes. He was made Baron and promoted General of Division, but was killed at the siege of Cadiz in 1810.

Napoleonic cannon fired four sorts of projectile. Most common was the iron roundshot, whose weight defined the piece. The 12-pounder ball was 11.7cm (4.6 inches) in diameter: it had a maximum range of some 1,650m (1,800 yds). Canister or case-shot had numerous balls contained in a tin container which burst at the cannon's muzzle: a 12-pounder light canister contained 112 balls, and the heavy version had 46 larger ones. The heavy canister of a 12-pounder could reach out to 550m (600 yds). Common shell, the preferred projectile for howitzers, was an iron globe filled with powder ignited by a fuse. Fuses were unreliable, making it dangerous to fire over one's own troops, and shells often burst into a few large pieces which limited their lethality. A type of British shell, called shrapnel or spherical case contained musket balls as well as a bursting charge, and was intended to explode in the air above its target. Carcass, also fired from howitzers, ignited to produce illumination or to set fire to combustible targets.

Foot artillery, whose gunners marched alongside their horse-drawn pieces, and which accompanied infantry formations, might achieve 15–25km (10–15 miles) a day, and more in emergencies. Horse artillery accompanied cavalry, and the gunners were all mounted on ammunition limbers or on horses to maintain speed. Although Napoleon's artillery was rarely decisive on its own, there were times when its concentrated fire shook opposing infantry so badly as to render it incapable of resisting a French onslaught.

This was Napoleon's plan for Waterloo, his last battle, and had the ground been firm enough to permit him to get his great battery of 84 12-pounders into action sooner, the fortunes of the day might have been different.

CHAPTER FOUR

THE ITALIAN
CAMPAIGN

**In the aftermath of Vendémiare, Napoleon
was promoted to General of Division and
appointed Commander of the Army of the
Interior. But his real interest lay in Italy.**

Here, the French and Austrians were in sharp contention, and he
repeatedly criticized Schérer's conduct of operations there, inducing
the Directory to give him command of the Army of Italy, replacing Schérer
in March 1796. The strategic plan had been established by Lazare Carnot,
the engineer officer and mathematician turned Republican politician and
strategist: France, assailed by numerous opponents, had to carry the war
into enemy territory; and Carnot planned to use five field armies to fight
a co-ordinated campaign in southern Germany and northern Italy.

In late March, Napoleon reached Nice, and assumed command of a threadbare army with just 37,000 effectives. He was 26, and some senior officers attributed his appointment to politics, thinking that his recent marriage to Josephine Beauharnais, former mistress of Paul Barras, was part of the plot. Napoleon lost no time in disabusing them. He jabbed forward and beat the Austrians at Montenotte on 12 April, but heavy fighting in the middle of the month was inconclusive. He regrouped, and on 21 April, took the well-stocked arsenal at Mondovi from the Piedmontese, persuading them to seek an armistice and freeing him to deal with the Austrians.

Napoleon crossed the River Po by sending Masséna and Sérurier to fix Austrian attention on Valenza while the rest of the army lunged eastwards to cross at Piacenza. Beaulieu, the Austrian commander, was shaken by the speed of the advance and fell back towards Cremona. On 10 May, Napoleon caught his rearguard at Lodi on the River Adda. Milan fell five days later, and the spoils of the city enabled Napoleon to pay his army in cash for the first time.

Napoleon had to deal with risings in Milan and Pavia before pushing Beaulieu along the shores of Lake Garda and gaining possession of the whole Lombard plain. The powerful fortress of Mantua, however, held out, and French communications were stretched thinly across recently conquered territory. At this juncture, Würmser arrived with Austrian reinforcements, collected Beaulieu's scattered forces and advanced on Mantua, down both sides of Lake Garda. Napoleon was in real trouble, with outlying detachments driven in and lines of communication cut: he had to raise the siege of Mantua. However, Augereau checked the Austrian advance at Castiglione on 5 August, enabling Napoleon to concentrate and defeat Würmser's main body. Napoleon again besieged Mantua, and then, moving at the lightning pace that characterized the campaign, triumphantly outmanoeuvred Würmser, who found himself blockaded in Mantua. In November, the Austrians committed two more armies under d'Alvintzi and Davidovich to a two-pronged attack, but Napoleon, now at the very height of his powers, jinked round d'Alvintzi's flank, secured the crucial bridge over the Adige at Arcola, and won a three-day battle

André Masséna (1756–1817)

A cabin boy before joining the infantry, Masséna retired in 1789 but re-enlisted and enjoyed meteoric promotion, becoming General of Division in 1793. He made a major contribution to the French victory in Italy, beat Suvorov at Zurich in 1799 and defended Genoa in 1800. Created Marshal in 1804, he commanded the *Grande Armée*'s right wing in 1807 and was made Duke of Rivoli. In 1809 his tenacity earned him the title Prince of Essling. But, repulsed by the British before the Lines of Torres Vedras in 1810, he never received another major command.

on 15–17 November that sent the third Austrian counter-offensive reeling back.

Duly reinforced, d'Alvintzi tried again, but was beaten at Rivoli on 14 January 1797, and Mantua surrendered on 2 February. Napoleon now faced a fresh army under the Archduke Charles, but had reached the Semmering Pass – from where his advance guard could glimpse the spires of Vienna – when an armistice was agreed in April. Though Napoleon's conduct of the campaign was not perfect, he had excelled in concentrating at the decisive point, and his personal courage, vital energy and inspirational words had made him the army's darling. It was a stunning debut.

CHAPTER FIVE

INFANTRY

The infantryman made up the most numerous component of any Napoleonic army, trudging the roads in rain or shine, and often deciding battles by the fire of his musket or the shock of his bayonet.

Most French foot-soldiers carried the 1777-pattern flintlock musket or its war production 1793 version. To load it, the soldier – taught the process in 21 drill-movements – bit open a paper cartridge, keeping the round lead musket-ball in his mouth. He trickled some powder into the priming-pan, and snapped the steel shut on top of it. Then he put the remaining powder into the muzzle, spat the ball on top of it, and rammed in the cartridge as wadding. To fire, he brought the musket up to his shoulder, thumbing the cock back as he did so. When he pressed the trigger, the cock shot forward: the flint gripped in its jaws hit the steel, striking a spark that ignited the powder in the pan and flashed through the touch-hole to fire the weapon.

But sometimes the flint would not spark, or the touch-hole was blocked by residue. Men had to replace flints and use a picker, hung from a cross-belt or button, to unblock the touch-hole. In heavy rain, priming-pans got soaked: on the Katzbach in 1813, in the rain, three-quarters of the muskets would not fire. A trained soldier could fire three rounds a minute, but for a line of infantry this might fall to four rounds in three minutes. Musketry was effective against a large target at 100m (110 yds) and dangerous at 200m (220 yds): bullets might carry up to 500m (550 yds), but at this distance they rarely killed. Rifles, whose grooved barrels gave them better range and accuracy, but a slower rate of fire, were carried by some skirmishers.

In 1789, there were 101 French regiments of infantry with royal or regional titles. After the Revolution these became numbered, and in 1793 they were abolished in favour of 198 demi-brigades, each with three battalions, one from the old army and two of volunteers. Numbered regiments – 90 line and 27 light – replaced demi-brigades in 1803, and by January 1813 there were 169 regiments, 133 of infantry of the line and the remainder light. Although light infantry paid special attention to skirmishing, the practical difference between these and line regiments diminished. Detailed organization varied, but a regiment, commanded by its colonel, contained two to four battalions, each under its chef de bataillon. Typically, a battalion might have six "centre companies" and two elite companies – a grenadier company and a light (voltigeur) company. Grenadiers, the biggest and bravest men, could spearhead an assault, or advance at the rear to buttress the faint-hearted. The light company contained the best shots, who often skirmished ahead of the battalion, using cover and firing independently. A company, in theory comprising 120 men, was commanded by a captain, with a lieutenant and a sous-lieutenant. Two to four regiments formed a brigade, and two or more brigades, often with a battery of artillery, comprised an infantry division. According to the 1808 organization, a battalion numbered 834 men plus a small battalion staff. In practice, however, a battalion's field strength early in a campaign was usually around 600, reducing as the campaign wore on. In 1811 in Portugal, for example, Masséna's battalions averaged around 350 men.

Training was based on the *Regulation of 1791*, which emphasized the methodical execution of drill movements. Eighteenth-century theorists had debated the relative merits of the line, which maximized firepower, and the column, the most expeditious means of moving troops cross-country, and which gave the best chance of breaking the enemy's line by physical and psychological shock. The emigration of many officers and the arrival of poorly trained volunteers meant that French infantry of the 1790s had little chance of adhering to the drill-book, but instead showed a natural aptitude for advancing in column, preceded by swarms of skirmishers, whose fire might unsettle the enemy and enable the column to put in a bayonet charge. Later, various forms of *ordre mixte*, with part of a unit in line and part in column, were widely used. It is not true to assert that the British always fought in line and the French in column, although their two-deep line (in contrast to the three-deep line of most other armies) did enable the British to make best use of their available manpower. Wellington showed particular aptitude for sheltering his lines behind the crests of hills or ridges, so that attacking French columns were often subjected to accurate close-range fire with little warning.

One colonel told the author Stendhal that in three years his regiment had put 36,000 men through its ranks. It was difficult to produce sufficient trained officers and NCOs. In 1811, Napoleon complained that he had found a sergeant with less than a year's service and 19 corporals with under two. "Repeat the order that no NCO will be appointed without three years' service," he wrote. Some infantry sent to Russia in 1812 did not understand how, when skirmishing "to use the rise and fall of the ground, but instead manoeuvred mechanically", and, as standards declined, generals often responded by using huge columns that maximized control and cohesion. In 1814, one general "could only move his troops in mass, when the officers and file-closers could keep them formed up".

E G Y P T   &   S Y R I A

**Secure in his domination of Italy, Napoleon
turned to the Mediterranean and Egypt in
a campaign intended to throttle Britain's
eastern commerce.**

In 1797 Napoleon dominated northern Italy, returning to France after peace was made with Austria at Campo Formio that October. He was lionized in Paris, and was delighted by his election to the Institut de France, a learned society comprising five academies, including the Académie française. Although he had little time for the Directors, he agreed with them on one main issue. The Directory was anxious to humble Britain, whose prime minister, William Pitt, was seeking to assemble a new anti-French coalition. Napoleon concurred: the British were "scheming and active" but if they were destroyed then "Europe is at our feet." Given command of the Army of England in early 1798, he decided that invasion was impossible without control of the sea. He concluded, however, that the capture of Egypt would be conclusive, enabling the French to invade India, or to lacerate the commerce upon which Britain depended. How this could be accomplished in the face of the British Royal Navy was never adequately explained.

With the expedition almost ready to leave, relations with Austria worsened, and Napoleon pressed the Directors to send him to dictate harsher terms than those previously imposed. When they baulked, he set off for Toulon, and on 9 May sailed aboard Vice Admiral Brueys's flagship *L'Orient*, his squadron part of a larger fleet of over 300 vessels carrying almost 37,000 troops. Napoleon paused to compel the surrender of Malta, and, fortuitously eluding a British fleet under Rear Admiral Nelson, began to disembark his army in Marabout Bay on 1 July. Exactly a month later, Nelson returned to find Brueys's fleet in Aboukir Bay and destroyed it at the battle of the Nile: Napoleon would have to fight with his lines of communication severed.

William Pitt the Younger (1759–1806)

The second son of William Pitt, Earl of Chatham, Pitt the Younger was called to the bar in 1780, became an MP in 1781, and Chancellor of the Exchequer the following year. He became Prime Minister in late 1783, and over 20 years of almost unbroken power strengthened his position with formidable oratory and skilled political manoeuvre. He hoped to avoid involvement in European war, but became an untiring opponent of revolutionary and then imperial France. He died, worn out, under the shadow of Austerlitz.

On 2 July, Napoleon's troops seized Alexandria, and he then set out on a desert march towards the Nile which brought his men to the edge of mutiny. The Mamelukes – ruling what was in theory a Turkish province – sent a detachment forward while the remainder concentrated near Cairo. Napoleon reached the Nile on 10 July, and on 13 July, there was a battle between French and Mameluke flotillas, won by the French

William Sydney Smith (1764–1840)

Smith was promoted to Lieutenant for bravery in 1780, became
a captain two years later and in 1792 was knighted for services
to Sweden. He helped burn the arsenal at Toulon in 1793, and,
though captured on a clandestine mission in 1796, escaped two
years later. Smith defended Acre in 1799, assisted Abercrombie in
Egypt, recaptured Capri for the Neapolitans in 1806 and destroyed a
Turkish fleet in 1807. In 1812–15 he was second in command of the
Mediterranean fleet. Quarrelsome, self-publicizing (and probably a
lover of the estranged wife of the Prince of Wales), Smith was a daring
officer with a flair for diplomacy. Napoleon said of him: "That man
made me miss my destiny."

when the opposing flagship blew up. The decisive clash came north-west
of Cairo on 21 July (the battle of the Pyramids). Murad Bey's cavalry
charged the French, formed up in great squares, and were beaten off
with huge loss. Napoleon entered Cairo two days later. On 11 August,
the Mameluke survivors were defeated at Salalieh, and Napoleon told
the Directory that "the country is under our control and the people are
becoming used to us".

In fact Murad Bey fought on, and Turkey's declaration of war
inspired a rising in Cairo. The Turks, encouraged by a British naval
detachment under Commodore Smith, prepared to counter-attack, and

Jean Baptiste Kléber (1753–1800)

Kléber was an architect who served as an Austrian officer before
enlisting in the revolutionary army, becoming a brigadier in 1793. He
helped suppress royalist risings in the Vendée, and played a leading
part in beating the Austrians in 1794–96. However, doubting his own
considerable abilities, he refused command of the Army of the Rhine
and went to Egypt. Taking command when Napoleon departed, he
signed the convention of El Arish in 1800, but he resumed fighting
when the Turks declined to ratify it, beating them at Heliopolis and
retaking Cairo, where he was assassinated.

Napoleon, never one to wait passively, set off through Sinai in February 1799. It took 11 days to take El Arish. Gaza fell without resistance, and Jaffa was stormed on 7 March, in a victory marred by the butchery of the town's garrison. Acre held out under Djezzar Pasha, encouraged by the arrival of Smith with reinforcements. Kléber, marching inland, smashed the Turks at Mount Tabor on 16 April, but the siege of Acre stalled, and in May Napoleon decided to fall back. On 25 July, he beat a Turkish army landed by the Royal Navy in Aboukir Bay. But the Directory had concluded that Egypt was no longer important, for Pitt had assembled a Second Coalition. Napoleon sailed for France on 22 August, leaving Kléber in command: it would be two years before the survivors returned home.

CHAPTER SEVEN

BRUMAIRE &

MARENGO

**"If it had not been for you English, I would
have been Emperor of the East", lamented
Napoleon in later life.**

British seapower may have wrecked his Egyptian adventure, which achieved none of its strategic objectives, but the evidence of French ambition actually hastened the formation of the Second Coalition against Napoleon. Although the expedition diminished the Directory's stature, it enhanced Napoleon's. His unexpected return in October 1799 affronted the Directors, who gave him what he called a "glacial reception". But, coming just after the dispatch announcing his victory against the Turks at Aboukir, it delighted the public, and Napoleon's journey from Fréjus to Paris was accompanied by wild enthusiasm.

Napoleon reappeared at a crucial moment. Masséna had just defeated the Russians in Switzerland, and an allied army would shortly be driven out of Holland. Royalist members of the Council of Five Hundred (the lower house of the legislature) had been expelled in 1797, and counter-revolutionary revolts in Brittany and the south-west had been suppressed. Although the Council's extremist neo-Jacobins aired the old revolutionary rhetoric, the capital's appetite for violent politics seemed sated. Yet if France craved stability rather than more revolution, the status quo offered few attractions to ambitious generals.

There were private tribulations. Josephine's spectacular adultery with a young officer, Hippolyte Charles, had exasperated Napoleon, and on his arrival in Paris he locked her out of his bedroom. Josephine and her children Hortense and Eugène noisily beseeched him to show mercy. Napoleon eventually opened the door and "their union ... was not again troubled", but Josephine now found her husband less pliable, and insistent that she break with her louche friends in "the Directory crowd".

Napoleon worked covertly with political supporters to develop his own role. Some, like Sieyès, wanted the executive strengthened at the expense of the legislature and needed a general to stage a coup. "You want power," said Foreign Minister Talleyrand, "and Sieyès wants a new constitution. Therefore join forces." Napoleon's brothers Joseph and Lucien intrigued, and on 25 October Lucien became president of the Council of Five Hundred. On 9 November (18 Brumaire), an alleged conspiracy provided the excuse to move the two legislative assemblies, the Council of Ancients and the Council of Five Hundred, to St-Cloud, outside the capital. Given command of the troops in Paris, Napoleon harangued 10,000 soldiers in the Tuileries gardens. On 19 Brumaire he

---

Jean Victor Moreau (1763–1813)

Moreau was training as a barrister when he joined the National Guard, and was General of Division in 1794, successively commanding the armies of the North, the Rhine and Moselle, the Sambre-et-Meuse and Italy. He supported the Brumaire coup in 1799, and won a major victory against the Austrians at Hohenlinden in December 1800. His ambitious wife may have led him to back Cadoudal's 1803 conspiracy, or Napoleon's jealousy of his considerable talent may have encouraged unjustified suspicion. The exiled Moreau went to America but in 1813 returned to Europe, to be mortally wounded at Dresden as adviser to the tsar.

---

went to St-Cloud, but panicked when confronted by furious deputies. Lucien told the soldiers that the deputies sought to murder their general, and Murat, who had commanded the cavalry in Italy and Egypt, led them forward. They burst into the chamber, and by nightfall there was a three-man "provisional executive" dominated by Napoleon. A new constitution was ratified by plebiscite in December, with Bonaparte as first consul, Cambacérès as second and Lebrun as third.

His political power secure, Napoleon turned his attention to military affairs. The French faced one large Austrian army in the Black Forest and another on the Upper Danube, with a smaller force in Italy. Napoleon compiled plans for an advance on Vienna, but the Austrians launched an unexpected offensive in Italy, and in May 1800, Napoleon took his army over the St Bernard Pass, reaching Milan on 2 June. Determined to bring General Melas to battle, Napoleon was caught off-balance on 14 June when the Austrians attacked part of his army at Marengo. He sent a desperate message – "come back, in God's name" – to Desaix, who arrived in mid-afternoon, and declared that the battle was lost but there was still time to win another. As his infantry counter-attacked, the younger Kellermann charged the Austrian flank, and within minutes the Austrians collapsed.

Marengo did not end the war, and it took Moreau's victory of Hohenlinden on 3 December to persuade the Austrians to sign the Peace of Lunéville on 9 February 1801. Britain agreed terms in October 1801 and confirmed them by the Peace of Amiens in March 1802. Napoleon, both victor and peacemaker, was appointed consul for life – sole head of state – on 2 August.

Louis Charles Antoine Desaix (1768–1800)

Desaix was an aristocrat (des Aix de Veygoux) and regular officer who supported the Revolution, though he was imprisoned for protesting against the king's dethronement. In 1796 he commanded the rearguard covering Moreau's retreat through the Black Forest, and then defended the ruined fortress of Kehl against the Austrians, capitulating only when all ammunition was expended. He did well in Egypt, earning the title "the just sultan" from the inhabitants of the province he administered, and was killed leading the decisive counter-attack at Marengo.

CHAPTER EIGHT

RULER &

LAWGIVER

**As Emperor, Napoleon remodelled the
French state, sweeping away the feudal
vestiges of the old regime and bestowing
on France an efficient bureaucracy and a
single code of law.**

In 1803 the Vendean leader Georges Cadoudal planned to assassinate
Napoleon. The plot failed and its participants were executed, although
Moreau (the victor of Hohenlinden), against whom evidence was weak,
was allowed to go into exile. To underline the seriousness of the regime's
response, the young Duc d'Enghien – heir to the Prince de Condé, head
of a collateral branch of the Bourbons – was kidnapped from the German
state of Baden, brought back to France and shot for being an émigré in
foreign service. All this helped create the climate in which the Senate,
gently prompted, proclaimed Napoleon Emperor on 18 May 1804: the

customary plebiscite confirmed his elevation. To win the Pope's approval, Napoleon went through a religious form of marriage to Josephine in private, and when he was crowned on 2 December, he was anointed by the Pope but placed the crown on his own head.

Napoleon had already begun the reconstruction of France. He emasculated the representative institutions he inherited, with a Senate, a Legislative Body, and a Tribunate – the latter abolished in 1807 for venturing mild criticism. The executive, in contrast, was strengthened enormously. Most ministries had been reorganized after the Revolution, and under Napoleon there were logically defined ministries of the Interior, Foreign Affairs, Finances, Justice, War, Marine and the Colonies, and Police, with a State Secretariat to co-ordinate and direct policy. There was, unsurprisingly, neither cabinet nor first minister.

The Council of State was the most influential new institution. Its members were chosen widely from distinguished men across the political spectrum: it prepared laws and regulations, formed a reservoir of senior officials for special tasks and subjected ministries to expert supervision and review. These supervisory duties eventually led to the creation of a corpus of administrative law, and the Council was to develop into what one historian called "the unshakeable corner-stone of French bureaucracy".

Powerful central institutions controlled local administration. Authority in a department lay in the hands of its prefect, appointed from and answerable to Paris, whose uniform betokened his status within a disciplined hierarchy. His sub-prefects, less gorgeously uniformed, were often local men, but had no electoral constituency and, like their master, were the government's creatures. These arrangements in part harked back to the *intendants* of Louis XIV, but the fact that the Revolution had felled a forest of medieval survivals permitted comprehensive centralization that the old regime, hedged about with feudal relics and customary laws, could never have achieved. When central government was strong, the new system worked well, but in his desire to destroy local power Napoleon removed regional counter-weights to instability at the centre.

Replacement of the varied laws of France by a single code had begun under the old regime and continued with the Revolution. Napoleon accelerated the process in 1800 by giving a group of distinguished

Charles Maurice de Talleyrand-Périgord (1754–1838)

Talleyrand was an aristocrat who became Bishop of Autun in 1788 and a radical member of the Estates-General the following year. Absences in London and the United States between 1792 and 1796 allowed him to avoid arrest during the Reign of Terror. He returned after Robespierre's fall to become Foreign Minister under the Directory and Consulate. Despite his role in helping Napoleon to the throne, he resigned in 1807 shortly after Tilsit, having become disillusioned over the years with Napoleon's exacting of harsh terms from the vanquished nations. He became a leader of the anti-Napoleon faction, re-emerging as Foreign Minister under Louis XVIII in 1814, and serving at the Congress of Vienna. His last major role was as King Louis-Philippe's adviser in the revolution of 1830.

lawyers five months to sort things out. It took until 1804 for the code to be agreed, but such was the measure of its success that all 2,281 articles could be contained in one volume. The code enshrined equality before the law, religious toleration and the rights of property, which was to be inherited equally by all legitimate children. The Code of Civil Procedure was more complex, and although the new Criminal Code seems draconian to modern eyes, it was a good deal more reasonable than, for example, British practice at the time.

Napoleon's Concordat with the Pope in 1801 – which enabled the latter to anoint the Emperor at his coronation – accepted that Catholicism was the religion of the majority, but placed bishops under prefectoral control and paid state salaries to clergy. Monastic orders were allowed back into France, but papal bulls could be published only with governmental assent. Although the church retained control of primary education, the new secondary system focused on elite *lycées*, boarding schools whose uniformed pupils were destined for the most important posts in the bureaucracy, backed by secondary schools whose education fitted pupils for lesser commercial and administrative positions. There were specialist higher schools for education, medicine, pharmacy, law and the army. Napoleon's administrative and legislative achievements outlived him, and many are reflected in France today.

CHAPTER NINE

U L M &

A U S T E R L I T Z

**The Peace of Amiens was only a pause in
hostilities, and in 1805 the Third Coalition
took the field against France, with Britain
providing its gold and seapower and both
Austria and Russia its manpower.**

The plan of the Austro-Russian allies emphasized operations in north
Italy, but was flawed by its complexity and divided command, and
was predicated on the Russians arriving in Bavaria by mid-October.
Napoleon's response was wholly characteristic. His *Grande Armée* was
massed at Boulogne on the Channel coast, ready to invade England, but
it became obvious that the naval superiority upon which this depended
would not be secured, despite Spain's entry into the war on the side of
France. Once this was clear (and in fact before the decisive naval battle
of Trafalgar was actually fought) Napoleon decided instead to launch

more than 200,000 men towards the Danube along parallel routes. He collected Bavarian allies en route, enveloping the leading Austrian army under Mack before the Russians could intervene, then went on to defeat the main allied armies. The operation hinged on Napoleon's use of *corps d'armée*, which would allow self-contained formations – varying in size from 14,000 to 41,000 men – to march separately but fight united. Subsidiary theatres were left to subordinates: Masséna would fix the Archduke Charles in northern Italy, St-Cyr would prevent an allied descent on Naples, and Brune would watch the Channel.

Karl Mack von Leiberich (1752–1828)

Mack joined the Austrian cavalry in 1770, became a protégé of Field Marshal Lacy, was ennobled and did well against the Turks in 1788–90, at the cost of a head wound with lasting effects. A successful Chief of Staff in Flanders in 1793–94, he then served as Commander in Chief of the Neapolitan army but was captured by the French. After escaping, he was unemployed until the war party at court needed a general to help oppose the Archduke Charles, who argued that Austria was not yet ready to resume hostilities and hoped to implement thorough but controversial reforms. Mack became the army's Chief of Staff, but his own hasty efforts at reform were only sketchily implemented when war came in 1805. Mack himself was forced to surrender at Ulm. The resultant court-martial sentenced him to death, but this was commuted, and he was soon released, to be rehabilitated in 1819.

Most of his men were already moving when Napoleon left Boulogne on 3 September, and his advanced guards crossed the Rhine between Strasbourg and Mainz on 15 September. Mack, blinded by French cavalry, had no idea what was about to burst upon him, and the French began to wheel south on 2 October, cutting in behind Mack and pushing forces eastwards to find blocking positions in case the Russians arrived. Mack managed to get some cavalry away, but he surrendered his encircled main body of 60,000 men at Ulm on 20 October. Napoleon had no intention of stopping, for there were still substantial Russian and

Austrian forces in the field, and there was every danger that Prussia, some of its outlying territory already violated by the French advance, would join the coalition.

Napoleon decided to march on Vienna, hoping that by threatening the Austrian capital he would induce his opponents to fight. With his leading cavalry snapping at Kutusov's rearguards, now falling back eastwards, Napoleon left Munich on 28 October, but soon discovered that Murat had mishandled the pursuit. Not only had this enabled Kutusov to get away, but it permitted him to savage part of Mortier's corps at Dürrenstein on 11 November. Vienna, reached by the French on 12 November, was undefended, but the allies broke clear of the city and took up a position near Olmütz, with secure lines of communication running east and north. The French, in contrast, were at the end of their tether, worn out by the long advance and with fragile communications stretching westwards. Napoleon knew that delay would make his enemies stronger, and might enable those Austrians falling back from Italy to join the fray. He needed a decisive battle, but if his enemies recognized this they might keep out of reach. Accordingly, he used both diplomatic and military means to suggest that he was hopelessly weak, apparently seeking an armistice while he summoned his outlying corps to join him as soon as possible.

On 1 December, the French army formed up 10km (six miles) west of the small town of Austerlitz, its left flank on the Brünn–Olmütz road and its right on the ponds near Telnitz, with the Pratzen plateau to

Nicholas Jean de Dieu Soult (1769–1851)

A private in 1785, Soult was commissioned with the Revolution, becoming Brigadier in 1794, and playing a leading role at Zurich and in Italy in 1800–01. Appointed Marshal in 1804, he struck the decisive blow at Austerlitz, taking the Pratzen Heights. He was created Duke of Dalmatia in 1808, but had mixed fortunes in Spain, though he skilfully defended France's borders in 1813–14. He was not comfortable as Chief of Staff during the Hundred Days, but returned triumphantly to royal favour in the 1830s.

its front. Much of the army was invisible to the allies, who planned to attack the French right before swinging north to cut their line of retreat. There would be a subsidiary attack in the north. The allied juggernaut lumbered forward before dawn on 2 December, but as the sun broke through, Napoleon launched Vandamme and St Hilaire against the Pratzen, no longer properly defended as the allies slid southwards, and gained possession of the vital ground in the very centre of the battlefield, cutting off the allied jab at the shoulder. His right flank held out, though under pressure, and his left checked the attack up the road. Napoleon strengthened his centre before striking hard south-eastwards. The allies lost 27,000 men, about a third of their strength: French casualties totalled 9,000. The news broke the spirit of British prime minister William Pitt, who was dead within eight weeks. On 26 December, Napoleon and Emperor Francis of Austria signed the Treaty of Pressburg, which, against French foreign minister Talleyrand's advice, took substantial territories away from Austria and imposed a severe financial indemnity.

W A R   A T   S E A

In a naval war of skirmish and blockade – punctuated by infrequent larger-scale fights – it was superior British seamanship and tactics that enabled the Royal Navy to emerge victorious.

The navies of the Napoleonic Age counted their strength in "ships of the line". These were three-masted sailing vessels mounting heavy guns – the whole reason for their existence – and they fought in line-of-battle, trading close-range broadsides with their opponents. There was little technological difference between opposing fleets, and so seamanship and tactics were of fundamental importance in enabling admirals to squeeze every morsel of advantage from wind and tide. Getting "the weather gage" of an opponent was highly desirable, and in 1794 Howe manoeuvred for days in the Atlantic to get upwind of the French before fighting and winning "The Glorious First of June", the first naval battle between the Royal Navy and the navy of revolutionary France.

Navies customarily fought in line: however, if both sides remained in line, although they might do fearful damage to one another, it was rare for battles to be decisive. Wooden warships had an astonishing capacity to absorb punishment. Fire followed by explosion in the ship's magazine was what finished *L'Orient* at the Nile and *Achille* at Trafalgar. Capturing an opposing vessel usually required it to be boarded, almost impossible to achieve in linear battle. But British admirals were increasingly prepared to change the rules: at Camperdown in 1797, Duncan broke the Dutch line, capturing nine of their 16 ships of the line.

Pierre Charles Jean Baptiste Silvestre de Villeneuve (1763–1806)

Villeneuve joined the French navy in 1778. Promoted Rear Admiral in 1796, he fought at the Nile, and his was one of the two major vessels to escape. Captured on Malta, he was soon released, and in 1804 he commanded the Toulon squadron as a Vice Admiral. Napoleon ordered him to break the blockade, lure the British away and then escort the *Armée d'Angleterre* across the Channel. After a promising start he missed his opportunity. Hearing that he was to be superseded, he risked battle unnecessarily and was defeated and captured at Trafalgar. He apparently committed suicide in France after his release.

Breaking the rules lay behind Nelson's great victory at Trafalgar. Early in 1805 Napoleon instructed Villeneuve to lure Nelson's blockading fleet to the West Indies, and then return to collect the Brest squadron before escorting his invasion barges across the Channel. Although Villeneuve succeeded in the first part of his mission, on his return to home waters he was unnerved by an inconclusive action with Calder, and sailed south to Vigo, moving down to join the Spanish fleet at Cadiz. Although there was no longer any strategic justification for battle, for the *Grande Armée* had by now moved eastwards, Villeneuve put to sea with 33 ships of the line on 20 October. When the fleets met the following day the British, with 29 ships of the line, were at a slight numerical disadvantage, but were infinitely superior in terms of ship handling and gunnery. Nelson broke the Franco-Spanish line in two places, bringing about a series of vicious close-range actions in which British skills were at a premium. Although Nelson was killed in the battle, his fleet captured no fewer than 17 ships, though two were subsequently recaptured and more lost in the storm that followed. It was a decisive victory, destroying any chance of a French invasion of Britain.

Horatio Nelson (1758–1805)

Nelson was a Norfolk clergyman's son who joined the navy in 1770. After service during the American Revolutionary War, he was on half-pay before commanding HMS *Agamemnon* in 1793. Having lost an eye at Calvi in 1794, he was knighted for his part in Jervis's victory of Cape St Vincent in 1797, but lost an arm later that year. He destroyed Brueys's fleet at the battle of the Nile in 1798, gaining a peerage, and the King of Naples made him a duke for recovering his capital in 1799. Instrumental in defeating the Danish fleet at Copenhagen in 1801, in 1803 he blockaded Toulon. After Villeneuve broke out on 30 March, 1805, Nelson eventually fought him off Cape Trafalgar, and was killed in the moment of victory. Slight, vain and charismatic, he was a leader and tactician of rare genius.

As Trafalgar shows, once a linear battle had become a mêlée, ships hammered away at one another at point-blank range: a British lieutenant recalled that he could have thrown a biscuit on to the enemy warships on either side of his own at Trafalgar. Captains strove to maintain a high rate of fire and to rake an enemy vessel through its poorly protected stern, and here superior skill told heavily. The Royal Navy, longer at sea and able to keep its crews exercised regularly, enjoyed a real advantage over its opponents, often confined to harbour. Moreover, assertions that British seamen were unwilling victims of press-gangs and subject to constant brutality are wide of the mark. Most British warships had well-disciplined, confident crews, welded together into lethal fighting machines. The disparity in casualties at Trafalgar was shocking: the captain of the French *Fougeux* reported that three-quarters of his men were hit, and the Spanish *Santisima Trinidad* – with 136 guns the largest ship on either side – had 400 men killed and 200 wounded. In contrast, Nelson's flagship *Victory*, the hardest-hit British ship, lost 57 killed.

Battle on this scale was rare, and the Royal Navy's victories did not give it anything that it had previously lacked, for it consistently enjoyed command of the sea. It was usually not in the French interest to risk a major clash, for French possession of what theorists were to term "a fleet in being" tied down the bulk of the Royal Navy's strength without risk. For all the drama of a battle like Trafalgar, British maritime strength was generally used in blockade, which made it difficult for shipping to enter or leave French-controlled ports. Alfred Thayer Mahan, the American theorist of naval seapower, was in essence correct to write how: "Those far distant, storm beaten ships, upon which the Grand Army never looked, stood between it and the dominion of the world."

Yet the British did not have things all their own way. French naval vessels or privateers (private warships with a government's "letter of marque") often escaped from blockaded ports to wreak havoc on merchantmen. Although the damage done by these commerce-raiders was irritating – 2,861 British merchant ships were lost to enemy action between 1793 and 1800 – it was not decisive. The threat posed by French commerce-raiders never approached the damage done to Britain by U-boats in the two World Wars. In contrast, the prefect of the Lower Seine glumly reported in 1811 that: "Commerce is non-existent: it cannot prosper without maritime peace."

N A P O L E O N ' S

A R T   O F   W A R

**A contradiction lies at the heart of
Napoleon's generalship.**

On the one hand, he had undertaken a painstaking study of military theory, and recommended "deep thought as well as deep analysis". On the other, much about him went beyond the rational: "I have fought sixty battles and I have learned nothing which I did not know at the beginning." He rejected formulaic schemes, maintaining: "I have never had a plan of operations." Yet he was meticulous in his study of maps and detailed information, and wrote: "I am accustomed to thinking out what I shall do three or four months in advance, and I base my calculations on the worst conceivable situation." In short, Napoleon's teeming brain wove together intellect, instinct, experience and intuition to an unusual degree.

Napoleon never wrote systematically on the art of war, and his multi-volume *Correspondance* can be variously construed, with consistencies being counterbalanced by contradictions. In part this is because he did not wish to tell his enemies – or his subordinates either – quite how he operated; in part it was, as the distinguished Napoleonic scholar David Chandler observed, "that his genius was essentially practical rather than theoretical" and in part it reflected the tendency – not confined to great generals – to remember things as they might have been and not as they really were. His many interpreters added their own gloss to phrases in which Napoleon, writing in a language whose complexities he never fully grasped, may not necessarily have invested much importance.

The essence of Napoleon's generalship was a desire to seek out the enemy's army and to break it, thus – as he hoped – depriving the hostile state of the means of resisting him. In 1797 he affirmed: "There are in Europe many good generals but they see too many things at once. I see only one thing, namely the enemy's main body. I try to crush it, confident that secondary matters will then settle themselves." If this approach often worked, perhaps most effectively in the case of Prussia in 1806, there were times, most dramatically in Russia in 1812, when it did not.

Napoleon had no doubt that battle lay at the heart of war. Like the eighteenth-century theorist Guibert, whose works he admired, he rejected the notion of cautious campaigning sprinkled with sieges: "It is upon the field of battle that the fate of fortresses and empires is decided." He was amoral, arguing that "In war all that is useful is legitimate," and harsh utilitarianism characterized his approach to the losses that battle inevitably produced. He warned the Austrian statesman Metternich that: "A man like me troubles himself little about the lives of a million men." Yet there were moments when common humanity broke through, and after the battle of Eylau in 1807 he admitted to Josephine that "This is not the pleasant part of war."

Napoleon generally conceived an offensive plan based on detailed study, but ensured that there were many alternatives in case the master-plan foundered. He emphasized the security of his forces, so that an enemy would find it hard to glean intelligence, and at the same time sought to mystify and confuse his opponents. Speed was of the essence ("I may lose a battle but I shall never lose a minute"), for Napoleon appreciated the need to maintain a higher tempo than his enemy, who consequently lost freedom of action. He sought to concentrate against the decisive point, and some commentators wasted their energies on debating whether this was the enemy's strongest or weakest point. It might be either, depending on circumstances: what mattered was breaking the enemy's equilibrium, and then "the rest is nothing". He often wrote about the importance of the moral as opposed to the material, perhaps most usefully in 1808: "In war, three-quarters turns on personal character and relations; the balance of manpower and materials counts only for the remaining quarter."

The *corps d'armée* system enabled him to practise his three favourite strategic concepts. The *"manoeuvre sur les derrières"* ("advance of envelopment") embodied pinning an enemy army to its position while he struck at its flanks or rear. In "the strategy of central position" Napoleon sought to place himself between two opponents and to switch forces to defeat each in turn. Lastly, in "strategic penetration", Napoleon moved swiftly through an enemy's defensive cordon to seize a centre of operations from which he could execute another strategic ploy as the situation permitted. These were ideas rather than formulae, and it was in their combination that Napoleon showed his real genius.

CHAPTER TWELVE

THE JENA CAMPAIGN

Jena ranks with the "blitzkrieg" campaigns of the twentieth century as an example of speed and decisiveness.

Napoleon's victory at Austerlitz left Prussia's King Frederick William III, who had planned to join the war in the event of the expected allied triumph, in an impossible position. Napoleon imposed harsh terms on Prussia, depriving it of territory and drawing it into his network of alliances designed to increase the isolation of Britain. Not all Prussians would accept this, and a patriotic party coalesced around the strong-minded Queen Louise, who Napoleon described as "the only real man in Prussia". News that Napoleon planned to violate his recent agreement, as well as early stirrings of pan-German nationalism, edged the Prussians towards war. The Prussian army enjoyed a high reputation, but as Clausewitz, later a well-known military theorist but a regimental adjutant at the time, observed: "behind the fine facade all was mildewed".

Louis Nicholas Davout (1770–1823)

Davout was an aristocratic cavalry officer who embraced the Revolution although his career during it was chequered. A general in 1793, he served in Egypt before commanding the Consular Guard. Created Marshal in 1804, Davout was a model corps commander, with his skilful victories at Auerstadt (1806) and Eckmühl (1809) making him Duke and Prince respectively. He was tough and uncompromising ("the Iron Marshal") and probably had the ability for independent command. But Napoleon, who respected his talents, did not want too brilliant a subordinate, and never gave him the chance.

In August 1806, the Prussians and their Saxon allies drew up three field armies with the intention of attacking the French, who were deployed across a wide sweep of southern Germany. One army under Brunswick concentrated between Naumberg and Leipzig; another, under Hohenlohe, was around Dresden, and a smaller force, under Rüchel and Blücher, gathered at Mühlhausen and Göttingen. In all, the Prussians disposed of about 171,000 men and 300 guns. Before they had properly embarked upon a projected advance on Würzburg, they heard that Napoleon was already on the move, apparently making for Saxony. They then decided to mass west of the Saale, aiming to threaten Napoleon's left flank, and the impetuous Hohenlohe seized the opportunity to push part of his army well forward.

Napoleon had concluded that his aim must be to beat the Prussians before the Russians, who had not sued for peace after Austerlitz, could intervene. He decided to concentrate behind the Thuringerwald, in the area Bamberg–Forcheim–Bayreuth–Kronach, and then to move towards Leipzig with his army in three mutually supporting columns totalling some 180,000 men. He called the formation *le bataillon carré*: it would be able to meet attack from any direction, or to concentrate swiftly and fall on an opponent. There were to be diversions up the Rhine to keep the Prussians guessing.

On 10 October, the French met Hohenlohe's leading detachment, under Prince Louis Ferdinand, at Saalfeld. The prince was killed in action while striving to prevent the collapse of his outnumbered force, and the news of his defeat induced Hohenlohe to fall back on Jena. Brunswick and Frederick William, meanwhile, determined to concentrate on Weimar. Although Napoleon's light cavalry, moving ahead of his columns, did their best to keep him informed, he was still not certain of the Prussians' dispositions, and the imminent climax of the campaign was overshadowed by the fact that while Napoleon knew that there was a substantial Prussian force around Jena, the bulk of the Prussian army, with Brunswick himself, was actually further back at Auerstadt.

Early on 14 October, Napoleon attacked what he thought was the main Prussian army on the high ground just north of Jena, having sent Davout and Bernadotte on a wide right hook against the Prussian flank and rear. There were two distinct clashes that day. Napoleon, with some 96,000 men, beat the 66,000 Prussians and Saxons facing him in a hard-fought battle in which the Prussians showed their old inflexible valour, but were no match for the French ability to concentrate superior numbers or for their tactical flexibility. At Auerstadt the outnumbered Davout – controversially unsupported by Bernadotte, who got on badly with him – took on Brunswick himself, with only 27,000 Frenchmen to perhaps 50,000 Prussians, and defeated him in a sparkling display of dogged courage and fluid tactics.

Napoleon exploited this double victory remorselessly. Davout led his corps through Berlin on 25 October, and over the next few weeks surviving Prussian field forces and garrisons were snapped up. Stettin fell in late October and Hamburg the following month: a few survivors crossed the Oder to meet the Russians. The Prussian army, which had for so long set the standard to which many others aspired, had been comprehensively trounced.

CHAPTER THIRTEEN

GRANDE ARMÉE

The *Grande Armée* was a huge multinational force, furnished with a complex command apparatus, but all designed to serve Napoleon's directing will.

The armies of the Republic had geographical titles like the Army of the North, the Army of Reserve and the Army of Italy. The same principle continued under the Empire, but France's main army, usually under Napoleon himself, was often titled *La Grande Armée*, although the phrase now does duty to describe the French army of the era more generally. Yet the *Grande Armée* was not simply French. In the 1805 campaign, the reserve corps contained a division each of Bavarians, Württembergers and Badeners, and in the army that invaded Russia in 1812, there were Austrians, Badeners, Bavarians, Croats, Dutch, Hessians, Illyrians, Italians, Mecklenbergers, Neapolitans, Poles, Portuguese, Prussians, Saxons, Spaniards, Swiss, Westphalians and Württembergers, to say nothing of men from the Grand Duchy of Berg and smaller German principalities.

Some states produced contingents of proven reliability. The Poles had an affinity for Napoleon, largely because he had restored their country, thrice partitioned between greedy neighbours, in the form of the Grand Duchy of Warsaw. It was the Polish *1er Chevau-Légers Lanciers de la Légion de la Vistula* who struck such a devastating blow to Colborne's British brigade at Albuera in 1811. At the other extreme, Prussian co-operation was rarely more than grudging, and it was the Prussian General Yorck's decision to conclude the Convention of Tauroggen in December 1812 that began the disintegration of the alliance structure which Napoleon had imposed on Europe.

At the centre of the whole polyglot and polychromatic organization was the *Maison Militaire de l'Empéreur*, Napoleon's military household, with its three key figures: Berthier, Chief of Staff; Duroc, Grand Marshal of the Palace, responsible for the organization of the household; and Caulaincourt, Master of the Horse, who oversaw all matters equine, from the organization of the stables to messengers and escorts. A handful of senior generals, the official aides-de-camp, stood ready to take on special tasks, and young orderly officers were on hand to carry messages. The Emperor's personal *cabinet* included three private secretaries, who were expected to take down orders by day or night. The topographical office, headed by the methodical Bacler d'Albe, produced maps and maintained a situation chart.

Napoleon often rode out with his small headquarters, consisting of Berthier, Caulaincourt, the duty marshal, two aides-de-camp, two orderly officers, an equerry, a page carrying the Emperor's telescope, a cavalryman with a portfolio of maps and a pair of compasses, the Mameluke Roustam – his personal bodyguard, a former slave who had been given to Napoleon as a gift in Cairo – a groom, and an interpreter. Four squadrons of Guard cavalry followed close behind. Napoleon sat in a light carriage for longer journeys, and for more substantial trips used a special post-chaise, with a folding bed, desks and bookshelves – and even concealed diamonds in case his imperial bubble burst.

The army's headquarters was much bigger (3,500 officers and 10,000 men in 1812) and comprised Berthier's private staff and private office, and the general staff of the army, divided into three loosely defined

Louis Alexandre Berthier (1753–1815)

Berthier entered the army as a geographical engineer in 1766 and rose rapidly to Lieutenant-Colonel. Suspended in 1792–95, he was then re-employed as Chief of Staff to the Army of Italy, beginning a relationship with Napoleon which was to last until 1814. His real skill was as Chief of Staff, interpreter of his master's genius: he lacked talent for independent command. Napoleon, who made him Prince of Neuchâtel, was furious when he defected to Louis XVIII in 1814. In 1815, apparently morose at missing the Waterloo campaign, he jumped – or perhaps was pushed – from a window.

branches, one responsible for operations, one for food, accommodation and hospitals, and the third for prisoners of war, conscripts and military justice. This was not a headquarters in a modern sense: there was duplication and repetitive office work, and nobody – from Berthier downwards – was permitted any initiative: the whole apparatus existed to serve Napoleon's directing will.

Napoleon worked an 18-hour day on campaign, responding to the previous day's reports in the small hours, sleeping briefly before dealing with routine work (some of it non-military, for he was as much of a centralizer as head of state as he was as a general), orders and dispatches in the morning, and riding to visit units in the afternoon. This pattern of work produced a pulse of daily activity, with corps commanders receiving written orders from gallopers in the morning, and acting on them before submitting their reports at nightfall. Napoleon was capable of dictating several sets of orders at the same time. It was a style of command that made it hard to know if a subordinate really understood the essence of a plan: nowhere was this more marked than in the ambiguous orders sent to Grouchy before Waterloo.

Personal visits were scarcely less important than written orders. Napoleon was a fine – if somewhat theatrical – communicator, and his soldiers treasured praise and were distraught by rebukes. If his headquarters provided the mechanical impulsion that drove the *Grande Armée* along, it was the glimpse of a squat figure in a grey riding-coat, and the sound of language that could make a grenadier blush, that lifted its soldiers' spirits.

CHAPTER FOURTEEN

BERLIN TO TILSIT

Napoleon's crushing victories at Eylau and Friedland were crowned at Tilsit, where he dictated terms to the Russian tsar and Prussian king.

At Jena-Auerstadt Napoleon had won a battle but not the war. The King of Prussia was safe in Königsberg, Russia was safe in Königsberg, Russia was hostile, and though Austria was neutral, her quiescence could not be guaranteed. Napoleon attributed this Fourth Coalition's survival to British gold, and in November 1806 he signed the Berlin Decrees, ordering the closure of continental ports to British goods, the beginning of what was to become known as the Continental System. Britain responded in early 1807 with Orders in Council that declared France and her allies to be under blockade: neutral vessels intercepted with contraband were liable to seizure.

In late November 1806, Napoleon pushed eastwards on a wide front, taking Warsaw on 28 November, and establishing himself a central position from where he could deal with Bennigsen's Russians as they appeared. But an attempt to encircle them north-east of Warsaw in December misfired, and in early February 1807, Napoleon narrowly failed to catch Bennigsen on the River Alle. Despite atrocious weather, when the Russians paused at Eylau on 7 February, Napoleon concentrated to attack them. The battle began that day with a struggle for Eylau, although we cannot tell if this was Napoleon's original intention.

Pierre François Charles Augereau (1757–1816)

The son of a domestic servant, Augereau served in the ranks of the French, Prussian and Neapolitan armies, and practised as a fencing master before joining the National Guard after the Revolution. Commissioned in 1793, he shot to prominence by helping Napoleon win Castiglione in 1796, and later took it as his ducal title. Augereau was created Marshal in 1804, and served widely as a corps commander, often showing dash and tactical flair, although suffering heavy casualties at Eylau in 1807. He rallied to the Bourbons in 1814, denouncing Napoleon as a tyrant. He was rebuffed by Napoleon in 1815 but also offended the Bourbons, and died without official employment.

Most soldiers of both armies spent a miserable night in the open and the following morning the French attacked in flurries of snow, initially outnumbered, but with both armies rising to about 75,000 as reinforcements arrived. Napoleon hoped to use Davout's corps, still on its way, to turn Bennigsen's left flank, and attacked the Russians' centre to pin him to his position while the manoeuvre took place. But the Russians engaged both Napoleon's flanks before Davout was ready, and the Emperor sent Augereau against the Russian centre left. Augereau's troops lost direction in the snow and marched straight into a massed Russian battery which halted them before infantry counter-attacked, sweeping the survivors back. Napoleon turned to his cavalry, and in late morning ordered Murat to charge the masses of Russian infantry who were pressing in on Eylau.

This charge tore deep into the Russian centre and bought valuable time. The advantage swung first to the French, as Davout pushed back the Russian left, and then to the Russians, as Lestocq's Prussians fell on Davout's open flank. But at the very end of the day, Ney's corps came up on the French left, and although it was beaten back it put new heart into Napoleon's men. That night, Bennigsen decided to retreat, having lost perhaps 15,000 men, fewer than the French, whose losses may have totalled 25,000. Even Ney was shocked by the sight of the battlefield: "What a massacre! And without a result."

Marie Walewska (1789-1817)

Marie was married to the much older Count Walewski. When she met Napoleon in 1807, her golden hair made an immediate impression. Invited to an imperial ball in Warsaw, she received an ardent note from Napoleon immediately afterwards. Some Polish patriots pressed her to yield so as persuade him to treat their country equitably, and he assured her: "Your country will be dearer to me when you take pity on my poor heart." They became lovers, and she bore him a son, Alexandre. There was real affection in the relationship, and she visited Napoleon on Elba. Marie remarried in 1816 and died in childbirth in Paris: her heart is buried there, but her body was returned to Poland.

Napoleon put his men into winter quarters, and contemplated his next move. Reinforcements were needed to make good the losses: some conscripts of the Class of 1808 were called up 18 months early, and lads of the Class of 1807 began to arrive. Lefebvre was sent to besiege Danzig, taking it in May, but in June the French had the worst of a major action at Heilsberg on the Alle. Then, deducing that Bennigsen was making for Königsberg (then held by Lestocq's Prussians), Napoleon planned a wide encircling movement. However, he misjudged Bennigsen, who determined to attack Lannes's corps at Friedland, south-west of Königsberg, before help could arrive. Lannes held Bennigsen in play on the morning of 14 June, and late in the afternoon Napoleon was strong enough to attack. Although a French cavalry attack failed to break the last Russian resistance, the results of the day were impressive: for the loss of 8,000 men the French had killed or wounded almost 20,000 Russians.

Napoleon and Tsar Alexander met – with the King of Prussia as an uneasy member of the trio – at Tilsit on the River Niemen, the border between Russia and Prussia, in late June and early July. Prussia was the real loser in their deliberations, emerging shorn of most of her outlying dominions and paying a huge war indemnity. Napoleon turned westwards, confident that he had real personal understanding with the tsar: it was perhaps the apogee of his success.

CHAPTER FIFTEEN

CAVALRY

**Napoleon built up a formidable cavalry force
– most notably of heavy cuirassiers – which
played a vital role on the battlefield, but
demanded considerable logistical support.**

There were three types of cavalry in the French imperial army. The cuirassiers were perhaps the most distinctive of all. Amongst the 25 regiments of heavy cavalry in 1799 was one that wore the cuirass, body armour then considered rather old-fashioned, and Napoleon's cuirassier arm grew from this small beginning. From 1802, cuirasses were issued more widely, with the first 12 regiments designated cuirassiers the following year. The thirteenth to eighteenth regiments became dragoons, and the remainder were disbanded and their men posted to the new cuirassier regiments. A thirteenth regiment was raised in 1809, and in 1810 a Dutch regiment became the fourteenth. Two regiments of carabiniers (heavy horsemen who had long before been named from the carbines they had carried when such things were uncommon) retained their title, but from 1810 were equipped as cuirassiers.

Antoine Charles Louis de Lasalle (1775–1809)

Lasalle was a nobleman who lost his commission with the Revolution, but then enlisted and was commissioned again. In Italy in 1796, he visited his mistress behind Austrian lines, fighting his way out when discovered, and at Rivoli he broke an enemy brigade by a charge against impossible odds. In 1806, he bluffed the fortress of Stettin into surrender, and at Medellin in Spain in 1808 he saved the day by a headlong charge. Lasalle maintained that any hussar alive at 30 was a blackguard, and was shot through the head charging Austrian infantry at Wagram aged 34.

Heavy cavalry existed to break opposing cavalry or infantry by the shock of their charge, and the cuirassier's breast- and back-plate, and fur-turbanned steel helmet with a tall brass comb was believed to give him an advantage in hand-to-hand combat. However, a British officer, who met cuirassiers at Waterloo, thought this an "encumbrance and inconvenience ... quite useless as protection to the man, when exposed to shot, shell or point-blank musketry – the head, throat and legs being unprotected and exposed also to the sure points of a good swordsman." Ironically, the cuirass, still worn on ceremonial occasions by British Household Cavalry, made its reappearance in the British army after the Napoleonic wars.

Eighteenth-century armies raised light cavalry for scouting and outpost work. The original French light cavalry were *Chasseurs à Cheval*, 31 regiments-strong by 1811. Hussar regiments, their men originally modelled on horsemen from the Great Plain of Hungary, also existed before the Revolution, and several irregular units like *Les Guides de l'Armée d'Allemagne* and *Les Hussards de la Liberté* were incorporated into the regular army. There were 10 hussar regiments by 1810, when a Dutch regiment became the eleventh: two more were raised in 1814. Polish lancers entered French service in 1807, and from 1811 there were six regiments of *Chevau-Légers-Lanciers de France* and two of Poles, with a ninth regiment, originally German dragoons, soon added.

Dragoons were a hybrid. They began as mounted infantry, but were well on their way to being cavalry proper, with 18 regiments in 1791 rising to 30, although in 1811 six of these were converted to lancers.

Dragoons wore green uniforms topped by a brass helmet with a leopard-skin turban, and carried musket and bayonet as well as sword. There were often too few horses to mount all troopers, and some went to war on foot, to be mounted if the opportunity came.

Cavalry regiments, like their infantry counterparts, were commanded by colonels, and contained around 550 men. Though organization varied, most had a small headquarters and eight troops, captains' commands of around 60 men apiece, usually grouped into four squadrons. The first troop of the first squadron was the *Compagnie d' Élite*, and often celebrated the fact by wearing fur busbies.

All this cavalry demanded the constant resupply of horses. In March 1805, only 700 of the 1,060 cavalrymen in Davout's corps had horses, and 300 men in each dragoon regiment marched on foot. The defeat of Prussia in 1806 enabled cavalry to be remounted from captures and requisitions, but the 1812 campaign in Russia was disastrous for horses as well as men, and although Napoleon's agents bought over 21,000 mounts in two months, there were repeated demands on France, with voluntary donations and requisitions. Supply rarely met demand: by February 1813 one remount depot had received 765 of the expected 2,500 cuirassier horses, 350 of 600 dragoon horses, and 277 of 700 draught horses. Lowering the required standards helped make up numbers but often put French horsemen at a disadvantage.

Joachim Murat (1767–1815)

Murat was the son of a village innkeeper and enlisted in the cavalry in 1787. Commissioned in 1792, he helped Napoleon administer the "whiff of grapeshot" to the Paris counter-revolutionary mob in 1795, was a brigadier in Italy, a General of Division in Egypt and was wounded leading the decisive charge at Aboukir. He married Napoleon's sister Caroline Bonaparte in 1800, was created Marshal in 1804, Grand Duke of Berg and Cleves in 1806 and King of Naples in 1808. A cavalry leader of extraordinary ability, Murat lacked any strategic grasp. He rejected Napoleon in 1814, was refused an audience in 1815, and died attempting to recover his kingdom. With characteristic style, he ordered the firing squad to spare his face.

CHAPTER SIXTEEN

NAPOLEON IN SPAIN

**Napoleon occupied Spain to buttress his
Continental System, but initial success against a
British expeditionary force created a black hole
into which badly needed French resources were
soon sucked.**

In December 1807, Napoleon promulgated the Milan Decrees, outlawing neutral shipping that visited Britain. His Continental System, already begun by the Berlin Decrees, had not frozen British trade. Portugal was prominent amongst its flouters, and Napoleon planned to invade it, not simply to close this loophole but to provide a springboard in case Spain, at this juncture nominally France's ally, needed showing a firm hand. Napoleon built up an army under Junot and issued an ultimatum to the Portuguese regent. Prince John was prepared to comply with all its terms save one, and that was enough for Napoleon. The Spaniards allowed Junot into their territory in September, and in October the Treaty of Fontainebleau formalized arrangements. Junot made excellent progress,

Joseph Bonaparte (1768–1844)

Joseph was Napoleon's eldest brother. He studied for the bar at Marseilles and carried out diplomatic assignments for the new regime before being made King of Naples. He was a thoughtful and humane ruler, but was placed on the Spanish throne in 1808. Although his natural affability made him friends (and the nickname "Uncle Joe"), opponents portrayed him as Napoleon's cats-paw and he resented his lack of genuine independence. He returned to his pretty estate at Mortefontaine in 1813. After Waterloo he emigrated to the USA, but came back to Europe in 1832.

passing Salamanca on 12 November and entering Lisbon on 30 November. However, a British squadron had spirited away Prince John, his court and the Portuguese fleet. Junot's men set about systematic looting so that the campaign might at least pay for itself.

Napoleon again considered invading Britain, but many of the invasion barges collected at Boulogne before Austerlitz had since rotted, and there was little chance of commanding the Channel. Instead, he decided to secure Sicily, send an army through Spain to Gibraltar and North Africa, thus severing Britain's grasp on the Mediterranean, and finally to dispatch a fleet to the east to wreck British trade. French troops in Spain secured key fortresses by a variety of ruses, and in May 1808 Napoleon forced King Charles IV and his son Ferdinand to abdicate, and bundled them, together with the influential royal favourite Manuel Godoy, to exile in France. Napoleon invited his brothers Louis and Lucien to assume the vacant throne, and when they declined, ordered another brother, Joseph, King of Naples, to Madrid, bestowing the throne of Naples on his brother-in-law and cavalry commander Joachim Murat.

Things had already gone wrong. On 2 May 1808, Madrid rose against its occupiers, and the insurrection spread. Many civil officials and military commanders feared the rising's populist streak, but provincial juntas encouraged resistance on behalf of the popular Ferdinand, the fatherland and the faith. The British quickly took advantage, repatriating a Spanish corps from the Baltic, and sending Wellesley to Portugal. He beat Junot at Vimeiro on 21 August, and the Convention of Cintra, signed

John Moore (1761–1809)

Moore came from a wealthy Glaswegian family and was commissioned into the infantry in 1776. He represented a Scots parliamentary seat until 1790, and also served in America, Ireland and the West Indies. Moore fought in the 1799 Dutch expedition and Egypt, before commanding a brigade at Shorncliffe on the British south coast. There he had a remarkable impact on light infantry training, and was knighted before serving in Sicily and Sweden. In 1808, he commanded British troops in the Peninsula, but was killed the next year at Corunna. We cannot tell how he might have developed as a general, but he deserves great credit for his work on light infantry. Wellington later commented to his military secretary: "You know, Fitzroy, we'd not have won, I think, without him."

by Wellesley and two senior generals who had superseded him, agreed that the French would be evacuated from Portugal in British ships. The Convention was deeply unpopular in Britain, for the French took away a good deal of their loot, and it almost cost Wellesley his career, but was a humiliation for the French. Even worse was the news that Dupont's corps had been encircled by Spanish regulars at Bailén in July and forced to surrender.

Napoleon determined to go southwards himself "to get the machine working again". He first travelled to Erfurt to meet the tsar, in an effort to ensure Russian quiescence during his absence, and then departed for Spain believing that he had settled matters behind him. In November, he burst like a whirlwind on the Spanish armies, and recaptured Madrid in early December. He was preparing to move on Lisbon, but a small British force under Moore had made a circuitous journey from Lisbon to Salamanca before striking at Valladolid. Napoleon thundered after him in late December, crossing the Guadarrama in snow and almost catching Moore as he withdrew to Corunna. Early in January 1809, Napoleon left for France, leaving Soult to complete the pursuit. Moore was killed as his army defended its evacuation port, but most of the British escaped. As Napoleon re-entered France he left behind him the Spanish ulcer, already gnawing bloodily into French manpower.

CHAPTER SEVENTEEN

NAPOLEON'S

FAMILY

**The Empire became a family affair as
Napoleon entrusted to his brothers
subordinate kingdoms in Holland and
Spain, but for his own heir, he had to
wait until 1811.**

Charles and Letizia Buonaparte had five surviving sons and three daughters. Charles died in 1785, but Letizia survived to become a dignified queen mother – "Madame Mère" – dying after Napoleon in 1836. Napoleon looked after his siblings, though with varying success: "My brothers are nothing except through me," he ranted. His eldest brother Joseph, born in 1768, studied for the bar, and carried out diplomatic duties in 1800-06, when he was installed as King of Naples. He was a humane and popular ruler, but in 1808 Napoleon summarily moved him to Spain. Even there his affability shone through, but he was in an impossible position, faced with a divided nation and a major war. Returning to France after the defeat at Vitoria in 1813, he emigrated to the USA after Waterloo, and farmed near Bordentown, New Jersey. He returned to Europe in 1832, and died in 1844.

Josephine (1763–1814)

Marie Josephine Rose Tascher de la Pagerie was born in Martinique. In 1779, she married the Vicomte de Beauharnais, a French general. She bore him two children, and after he was guillotined in 1794 had several lovers. She married Napoleon in 1796, narrowly escaping rejection after an affair. Josephine contributed greatly to the brilliance of the court, but, unable to bear Napoleon a child, was divorced in 1810, retaining the title of Empress. She may have been the only woman he really loved, and he reflected that everything began to go wrong after their divorce.

Lucien, born in 1775, was altogether more determined. He became a member of the Council of Five Hundred in 1798 and was elected its president just before the Brumaire coup, in which he played a leading part. He was successful both as minister of the interior and ambassador to Madrid but, offered the crowns of both Sicily and Spain on condition that he divorce his bourgeois wife, resolutely declined, and lived on his estate near Rome, where the Pope made him Prince of Canino. Lucien fell out with his brother when French troops were sent into Rome in 1810. The ship carrying him to America was captured by the British, and he spent the rest of the Napoleonic wars living as a country gentleman at Ludlow in Shropshire and Thorngrove in Worcestershire. He returned to Italy, where he died in 1840.

Louis was born in 1778, and served in the French army. After his marriage to Napoleon's stepdaughter Hortense, he became King of Holland in 1806. Hortense bore him two sons, the second of whom became Emperor Napoleon III, but the marriage was unhappy, as was Louis's time in Holland. He was rebuked by his brother for putting Dutch interests above those of France, and forced to abdicate in 1810.

Thereafter, as Comte de Saint Leu, he lived in Austria, Switzerland and Italy, preoccupied with his health (there were concerns about his mental stability) and his literary endeavours, and died in 1846.

The youngest brother, Jerome, was born in 1784 and served in the navy before emigrating to the USA, where he married Elizabeth Patterson in 1803. In 1807, Napoleon made him monarch of the new kingdom of Westphalia, having divorced him from his wife and married him off to Princess Catherine of Württemberg. He served as a corps commander, with mixed fortunes, for his attacks on Hougoumont cost Napoleon valuable time at Waterloo. He received his marshal's baton from his nephew Napoleon III, and died in 1860.

Marie Letizia Bonaparte (1750–1836)

Born Ramolino, of a family of minor Italian nobility which had long lived in Corsica, Marie Letizia married Charles Bonaparte in 1764, and bore 15 children, though only eight survived infancy. She moved to France in 1793, living modestly until Napoleon's rise changed her fortunes. Designated Madame Mère de Sa Majesté l'Empereur, a title she hated, she was cautious with her own money, arguing: "My son has a fine position, but it may not continue forever." She preferred Italian to French, which she spoke poorly, and died in Rome, financially secure but blighted by the early deaths of several offspring.

Elisa Bonaparte, born in 1777, became Grand Duchess of Tuscany. She had something of Napoleon's manner, and enjoyed reviewing troops from horseback. Pauline was born in 1780. She married General Leclerc in 1797, and accompanied him on an expedition to Haiti, where he died: she then married Camillo Borghese, a Roman prince, but complained bitterly when her husband was sent to govern Piedmont. She returned to Paris, and enjoyed a racy lifestyle. The sculptor Canova produced a nude sculpture of her, and when asked how she could bear to pose for it, allegedly replied that it was no problem because there was a fire in the studio. Caroline, born in 1782, married Joachim Murat, Napoleon's most successful cavalry commander. She became Grand Duchess of Berg when Murat was given a state in north Germany, and became Queen of Naples after his elevation.

Napoleon married the "sweet and matchless" Josephine de Beauharnais, widow of a guillotined general, in 1796. Her elegance and charm did much for Napoleon, who forgave her for a major affair, and he treated her children Eugène and Hortense as his own, making the former Viceroy of Italy and marrying the latter to his brother Louis. Josephine could not bear him an heir, and he divorced her in 1810 to marry the plump and pretty Austrian princess Marie-Louise, who duly presented him with a son in 1811.

Napoleon described his many affairs as "pastimes that do not in the least engage my feelings". His mistresses included the actress Mademoiselle George, the Polish beauty Marie Walewska – who bore him a son, Alexandre, who became a distinguished diplomat and statesman under the Second Empire – and the singer Giuseppina Grassini. The latter later enjoyed the favours of the Duke of Wellington, and reported him a better lover, which may suggest that in love, as in much else, Napoleon was deeply selfish.

CHAPTER EIGHTEEN

THE WAGRAM CAMPAIGN

**Napoleon returned from Spain in early
1809 to find that Austria, heartened by
news of French setbacks in the Peninsula,
had decided to renew the war.**

The Archduke Charles had almost completed a thorough reform of the army, now increased in size and organized on the corps system. Although himself a very competent commander, he was saddled with numerous second-rate subordinates, but there was little comparison between Austrian resolve in 1805 and its much-improved state in 1809.

Napoleon's immediate problem was manpower, and he solved it by prematurely calling up conscripts of the Class of 1810, emptying depots and military academies, and by heavy reliance on German allies. At the end of March, the *Grande Armée de l'Allemagne* was over 170,000 strong. Napoleon was confident that his opponents would waste too much manpower in north Italy, leaving him free to strike down the Danube towards Vienna, and he ordered Berthier to plan a concentration on

Ratisbon, with Donauwörth, further west, as an emergency alternative. In fact, the Austrians detached relatively few troops to Italy and Galicia, keeping almost 200,000 on the Danube. Charles, who favoured a bold thrust towards Ratisbon, which he hoped would unsettle Napoleon's allies, was persuaded to attack south of the river.

The Austrians attacked on 9 April without a formal declaration of war, but moved ponderously into Bavaria, and when Napoleon reached his army on 17 April and took over from the rather outclassed Berthier, he swiftly ordered a concentration behind the River Ilm. Although he had not fully grasped Austrian strength or intentions, over the next week Napoleon swung the campaign his way, winning a victory at Abensburg–Eckmühl on 20–22 April that left the road to Vienna open before him.

The chastened Charles withdrew into Bohemia, and Napoleon decided to press straight on for Vienna, hoping that the threat might produce a negotiated peace, or at least draw the Austrians back from Italy, where his viceroy and stepson, Eugène de Beauharnais, was under pressure from the Archduke John. Hiller's rearguard gave ground stubbornly, but the French entered Vienna on 13 May. Charles swung his army north of Vienna, picked up Hiller's corps, and on 21 May, with about 110,000 men, launched a surprise attack on the overextended French (who had just 23,000 men initially, rising to 73,000 on the second day) around the villages of Aspern and Essling, on the north bank of the Danube east of Vienna. The island of Lobau lay behind the crucial sector, with

Nicolas Charles Oudinot (1767–1847)

Oudinot was a private soldier in the royal army but shot up to command a brigade by 1794. He made his reputation fearlessly commanding a force of grenadiers during the Austerlitz campaign in 1805, and went on to command a corps, taking over from the mortally wounded Lannes at Essling and spearheading the attack at Wagram. He was created Marshal in 1809 and Duke of Reggio in 1810. Although he was one of the last to abandon Napoleon in 1814, after the second restoration he served the Bourbons loyally, commanding the 1823 Spanish expedition. Napoleon's fearless "Bayard of the army", Oudinot was wounded in action 22 times.

Jean Lannes (1769–1809)

Lannes was a dyer's apprentice who joined the army in 1792 and was swiftly promoted. He served with the Army of Italy, where Napoleon made him a brigadier, and was twice wounded in Egypt. He helped with the Brumaire coup, and in the Marengo campaign won the independent victory of Montebello, which later brought him his ducal title. Created Marshal in 1804, he was a distinguished corps commander, with tenacity and valour as his hallmarks: at Ratisbon he grabbed a scaling ladder when the assault faltered. Mortally wounded at Essling, his loss was much regretted by Napoleon.

a single bridge linking it to the main French forces on the south bank. The Austrians had the better of the first day's fighting, but on 22 May, the reinforced French recaptured Aspern before Lannes's corps put in a formidable attack between it and Essling. This was narrowly checked by Charles at the head of his reserve, and, as Austrian pressure on the bridgehead grew, Napoleon realized that he would have to fall back across the river. Although losses were equal, at around 22,000 for each army, French prestige had suffered a palpable blow.

It was not until 5 July that Napoleon attempted to avenge himself, and he did so by concentrating opposite Lobau island and feinting along the river to distract Austrian attention. By that evening the French were north of the river, forming a wedge between the Danube and the Russbach, though they had not broken the Austrian line. At Wagram on 6 July, initial Austrian attacks gained ground, but were rolled back: the only thing that could now compromise Napoleon would be the arrival on his left flank of the Archduke John back from Italy, but he did not appear. Macdonald's corps was terribly mauled attacking the Austrian centre left, but Charles decided that the day was lost and ordered a withdrawal.

The battle of Wagram had cost the Austrians over 37,000 casualties to at least 32,500 French. It was not a triumph like Austerlitz or Jena, but was enough to force the Austrians to make peace. The Treaty of Pressburg, signed that December, deprived Austria of some territory, forced her to pay an indemnity and restricted her army to 150,000 men.

Jacques Louis David's painting of Napoleon, then First Consul, crossing the Great St Bernard Pass on 20 May 1800, transforms him into a romantic hero. Engravings on the rocks at his feet link him with Hannibal and Charlemagne.

This contemporary engraving of the execution of Robespierre is intended to portray the struggling victim in an unfavourable light. Those executed were in fact strapped to a plank, and Robespierre's jaw had already been horribly mangled.

Antoine-François Callet, *Portrait of Louis XVI*, 1779.

The "whiff of grapeshot": Napoleon's guns disperse the mob outside the Church of St Roche on 5 October 1795.

At Montereau on 18 February 1814, the arrival of the Guard artillery tilted the balance of firepower in French favour, and Napoleon personally led his artillery forward onto a captured ridge dominating the enemy position. He is best remembered for dismounting to lay a gun himself.

Napoleon and Empress Marie-Louise visiting the foundry at Liège. Although Napoleon took a close interest in gun founding, battlefield losses of guns after 1812 were so great that it was hard for manufacturers to keep up with them.

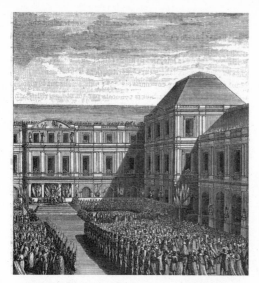

Napoleon is lauded after the Treaty of Campo Formio, formalized in October 1797, took Austria out of the war. It gave France control of Lombardy and improved her position on the Rhine, while Austria gained much Venetian territory.

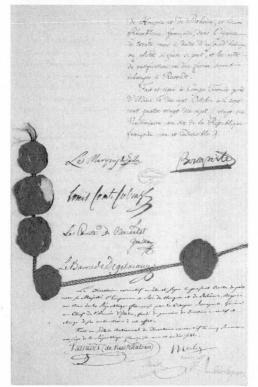

A signed and sealed manuscript of the Treaty of Campo Formio. Napoleon's signature, now spelt in the French fashion, is characteristically alone, on the right.

Antoine Gros's painting of Napoleon on the bridge at Arcola is more iconic than realistic. In fact a French officer told him "if you fall we are lost ... this is not your place", and shoved him into the comparative safety of the water.

Jean Auguste Dominique Ingres's iconic portrait of Napoleon enthroned as Emperor of the French, a supreme example of art serving the state.

A gold-embroidered black velvet binding of the first edition of Napoleon's *Civil Code*.

The title-page of the first edition of the Civil Code, published on 21 March 1804. This book has proved one of the more enduring Napoleonic achievements.

Horatio Nelson. Instrumental in defeating the Danish fleet at Copenhagen in 1801, in 1803 he blockaded Toulon. After Villeneuve broke out on 30 March 1805, Nelson eventually fought him off Cape Trafalgar, and was killed in the moment of victory. Slight, vain, and charismatic, he was a leader and tactician of rare genius.

Francisco Goya's *Dos de Mayo* depicts the execution of Spanish insurgents by a French firing squad following the Madrid insurrection of 2 May 1808.

The battle of New Orleans from the American viewpoint. The British attacked entrenchments defended by a mixture of regulars, militia and volunteers, including some pirates.

On 6 April 1812, Wellington stormed Badajoz. In the centre a mine explodes amidst troops attacking the main breaches, which are protected by chevaux de frise – timber studded with sword blades.

A caricature of the Congress of Vienna shows the victor dividing the spoils. The little King of Rome (left) urges Napoleon: "Papa, look after my share", although by now Napoleon had no chance of doing so.

A proclamation issued by Napoleon (already styling himself Emperor "by the grace of God and the constitutions of the State") on his return from Elba.

Paul Hippolyte Delaroche's painting *Napoleon at Fontainebleau, Brooding after Defeat in 1814.*

CHAPTER NINETEEN

THE SPANISH
ULCER
1 8 0 9 – 1 1

**British armies in the Peninsula enjoyed
widespread local support and were
sustained by the Royal Navy: Napoleon's
Spanish ulcer would prove incurable.**

Although the first British intervention in the Peninsula had ended in evacuation from Corunna, in April 1809, the British government, scenting the opportunity to use its command of the sea to sustain an expeditionary force at the periphery of French strength in the Iberian peninsula, sent Wellesley to command an army in Portugal. He first lunged north from Lisbon to beat Soult, and then marched into Spain with some 35,000 British troops to co-operate with Spanish armies in an advance on Madrid. Although the project eventually miscarried, as operations like this so often did, the French were sharply repulsed when Victor attacked the allies at Talavera in July. A grateful government ennobled Wellesley as Viscount Wellington. However, Wellington could not maintain himself in Spain, and fell back down his lines of communication into Portugal, where his engineers laid out the fortifications of the Lines of Torres Vedras to cover Lisbon in case of French pursuit.

William Carr Beresford (1768–1854)

The illegitimate son of the Marquess of Waterford, Beresford was commissioned in 1785, commanded the 88th Foot and distinguished himself against the Dutch at the Cape in 1806. Not a talented independent commander, he failed in an 1806 expedition to South America and was saved at Albuera in 1811 by the extraordinary performance of his infantry. He was a first-rate administrator, and after becoming Marshal of Portugal in 1809, overhauled the Portuguese army, enabling it to play an important role in Wellington's campaigns. He was created Baron in 1814 and Viscount in 1823, and when Wellington was Prime Minister, Beresford served as Master-General of the Ordnance.

Although British historians describe this conflict as "the Peninsular War", to the Spaniards it was "the War of Independence" and – start to finish – the French task was complicated by the fact that they were never able simply to concentrate on Wellington, but had to contend also with Spanish field armies and irregulars. The Portuguese army, too, remodelled with British help, became a useful adjunct to Wellington. This was a landscape where, as Napoleon observed, "small armies are beaten and large ones starve", and in which Wellington's mastery of logistics and British command of the sea were invaluable. The French, in contrast, tended to live on the country, worsening relations with a population deeply divided in its loyalties, with some supporting the affable King Joseph, Napoleon's brother, and others fiercely opposed to him. Although Joseph had perhaps 300,000 troops at his disposal, he struggled to conquer Andalusia and Catalonia, and to hold open lines of communication through guerrilla-infested countryside.

Juan Martin Diaz, "El Empecinado" (1775–1824)

Diaz, nicknamed "the stubborn one", was the son of a well-to-do farmer and volunteered to fight the French in 1793–95. In 1808 he joined the anti-French insurgency, and the central junta appointed him captain in 1809. His force grew to 5,000 men, and he had considerable success in the Valladolid area, often cutting the main Vitoria to Madrid road. Confirmed as a general in 1815, in the "Liberal Triennium" of 1820–23 he served as Governor of Zamora. Returning after exile in Portugal he was arrested, exhibited in an iron cage and hanged.

In summer 1810, Masséna took the Spanish fortress of Ciudad Rodrigo and Almeida, its Portuguese counterpart, and then moved south-west against Wellington. He was checked at Buçaco on 27 September, and then collided with the Lines of Torres Vedras. Wellington had left little but scorched earth in front of them, and Masséna eventually drew back to Almeida in the spring of 1811: he had lost perhaps 30,000 men. The campaign now centred upon the frontier fortresses of Ciudad Rodrigo, in the north, and Badajoz, in the south. On 3 May, Masséna attacked Wellington at Fuentes de Oñoro, south of Almeida, and was badly beaten. Further south, Wellington's subordinate Beresford was besieging Badajoz when a French army under Soult approached. Beresford drew off to block it, and on 16 May his British-Portuguese-Spanish force fought a bloody battle at Albuera. Although Soult was driven off, complaining in his dispatch that, "They were completely beaten and the day was mine, but they did not know it and would not run," Beresford lost 6,000 men to 8,000 French. His draft dispatch was so gloomy that Wellington told him to try again: "This won't do. Write me up a victory." Wellington resumed the siege of Badajoz, but could not take it. However, at the tail of the year his position improved as some French troops were withdrawn to fight the Spanish in Old Castile. It was also evident that Napoleon, with the Russian campaign looming, could spare no reinforcements for his brother. Wellington planned to open 1812 by taking Ciudad Rodrigo and Badajoz, which would then enable him to strike deep into Spain.

CHAPTER TWENTY

THE IMPERIAL

COURT

**Napoleon took being an emperor very
seriously, and told Madame de Rémusat,
one of Josephine's courtiers, that: "The
French Empire shall become the metropolis
of all other sovereignties."**

As first consul he spent much of his time in the Palace of St-Cloud, restored after its ransacking by revolutionary mobs, and extended it after he became emperor. On a bluff overlooking the Seine, it offered more privacy than the Tuileries, at the western end of the Louvre in the very heart of Paris. He enlarged the Louvre, erected a triumphal arch in its forecourt, completed the Cour Carrée at its eastern end, and built the north gallery running along the new road named, from an Italian victory, the Rue de Rivoli. The importance of the two palaces was underlined when Napoleon married Marie-Louise, after divorcing Josephine, in 1810: the civil ceremony was held at St-Cloud and the religious ceremony in the Louvre.

Marie-Louise (1791–1847)

Marie-Louise was the daughter of the Austrian Emperor Francis I.
Napoleon divorced Josephine to marry her in 1810. Having fathered
two bastards, he knew that he could produce a much-needed heir, and
Francis was content to give his daughter in a diplomatic marriage.
She bore Napoleon a son, the King of Rome, in 1811. The post-war
settlement gave her three Italian duchies which she ruled from Parma.
In 1821 she married Count von Neipperg, an Austrian veteran by whom
she already had two children, and married again after his death.

Of the royal palaces on the outskirts of Paris, Napoleon preferred
Fontainebleau to Versailles, because the latter bore the unmistakably
heavy stamp of Louis XIV, and it was at the foot of the horse-shoe
staircase at Fontainebleau that he said farewell to his guard on 20 April,
1814. Malmaison, in a bend of the Seine west of Paris, was bought by
Josephine in 1799. She loved its English rose garden, but Napoleon, who
regarded Great Britain as his chief adversary, preferred the new French
gardens he had constructed at St-Cloud. However, he bought a wooded
estate nearby, where he enjoyed hunting. Berthier, amongst his other
duties, was master of the hunt, but an attempt at a Corsican favourite,
a rabbit hunt, misfired when the creatures, mistakenly bought tame,
mobbed Napoleon in mistake for their keeper.

Géraud Christophe Michel Duroc (1772–1813)

The son of a nobleman, Duroc emigrated after the Revolution but
returned and became an artillery officer. He met Napoleon at the
siege of Toulon in 1793, and served as his aide-de-camp on successive
campaigns, being promoted General of Division in 1803. Appointed
Grand Marshal of the Empire in 1804 and Duke of Friuli in 1808, he
was responsible for the smooth running of the court. In addition, he
was a trusted diplomatic emissary and discreet procurer. When he
was mortally wounded near Bautzen in 1813, Napoleon, genuinely
distressed, broke off the action.

The splendour of the imperial court eventually yielded little to the old regime. Napoleon's glass-panelled coronation coach had a gilded frieze bearing medallions depicting the departments of the Empire, a veritable flock of gilded eagles and the crown of Charlemagne on a golden altar. But at this stage not all court life was starchy. On working days Napoleon would be awakened at 7.00 a.m., and his valet, Constant, would pour his bath. He often spent two hours in it, while a secretary read translations of English and German newspapers, and he would then be shaved. He spent the morning on correspondence and petitions, and sometimes interviewed petitioners personally. One worthy young man who had been denied admission to the *École Polytechnique* arrived at Malmaison and asked for an interview. Napoleon saw him, asked a number of questions, and duly ordered the director of the *Polytechnique* to admit him forthwith.

Napoleon lunched at 10.00 a.m., dined at 5.00 p.m., and had simple tastes in food: *poulet à la provençale* and potatoes fried in oil were favourites, and he liked to drink Gevrey-Chambertin, though he usually mixed it with water. Napoleon enjoyed playing cards, and cheated shamelessly. He did not share Josephine's passion for opera, and his singing voice was described by Laure Junot (the wife of General Junot) as "squealing" in contrast to "the fine sonorous accent of his speech". The theatre was a dominating passion: there were theatres at both St-Cloud and Malmaison, and such was his admiration for the playwright Corneille that he affirmed: "If a man like Corneille was alive today, I would make him my prime minister."

After his return from Tilsit, where he met an emperor to the manner born, Napoleon made etiquette more formal. Nobody could approach him without the approval of Duroc, responsible for the smooth running of the court, and also, more discreetly, for procuring ladies to satisfy his master's sexual whims. At Compiègne in 1810 a reception for distinguished guests was frozen into immobility when Napoleon stood wordlessly for a quarter of an hour: the easy days of General Bonaparte had been replaced by the frigid ceremony of the Emperor Napoleon.

CHAPTER TWENTY - ONE

THE   WAR   OF

1 8 1 2

**Relations between revolutionary France
and the fledgling United States were
uneasy from the start.**

Although the nations remained allies, a treaty of 1794 gave the British equal commercial interests in America, much to French annoyance. American negotiators were sent to Paris, but French warships and privateers snapped up American merchant ships suspected of carrying British goods in what was in effect an undeclared war. Negotiations were imperilled because the wily Talleyrand, Napoleon's foreign minister, demanded £50,000 as a gesture of goodwill ("the XYZ affair"), but in 1800 the Convention of Mortefontaine established American neutrality.

A day later, the Treaty of San Ildefonso affirmed that Louisiana (a vast tract of land much larger than the present state, approximately 22 per cent of the size of the present-day USA), ceded by France to Spain in 1763, would become French again once general peace was concluded. The Treaty of Amiens in 1802 constituted that peace, and French reacquisition of Louisiana left America exposed. If France actually reoccupied it, then – as President Jefferson observed – the USA would have little alternative but to ally with Britain. Early in 1803, Napoleon concluded that war would soon break out again, and it was important not to alienate the USA: he told Talleyrand to sell Louisiana. The Louisiana Purchase doubled the size of the USA at a cost of just $15 million, and, as Napoleon observed with satisfaction, "I have just given England a seafaring rival which, sooner or later, will humble her pride."

Napoleon's Berlin and Milan Decrees (known collectively as the Continental System) and the British response, the Orders in Council, were profoundly damaging to American commerce. Jefferson's Embargo Act of 1807 forbade the export of foreign cargo from American ports, and no sooner had James Madison become president in 1809 than it was replaced by the Non-Intercourse Act which allowed American shipping to trade with all except France and Britain. In 1810, Napoleon agreed not to apply his decrees to the USA, provided Britain also revoked her Orders in Council. This placed the onus on Britain, although no formal revocation was actually made by France at the time. In June 1812, when it was clear that the French had belatedly suspended the decrees, Britain followed suit. However, the "war hawks" in Congress, exasperated by the Royal Navy's habit of stopping American ships to search for deserters, had their way, and on 18 June America declared war on Britain before the news of revocation of the Orders in Council had crossed the Atlantic.

In 1812, the war on land went badly for the USA, with its three-pronged invasion of Canada failing utterly. At sea, however, the big American super-frigates like USS *Constitution* had the best of some celebrated actions, and warships and privateers lacerated British shipping. In April 1813, the Americans took York (now Toronto) and burned the government buildings; Perry's US squadron won a decisive engagement on Lake Erie, and a British force, accompanied by the Shawnee chief Tecumseh, was routed near Detroit in October. At sea, however, the British did better, protecting merchantmen by keeping them in convoy. HMS *Shannon* captured USS *Chesapeake* off Boston in the most remarkable single-ship action of the war, but American privateers, some striking into the North Sea, ravaged commerce.

James Madison (1751–1836)

Madison represented Virginia at the Continental Congress of 1780, and played a major part in framing the 1787 constitution. Mistrustful of the power of central government, he became a Jeffersonian republican, serving as Jefferson's Secretary of State before becoming president in 1809. In 1812 he allowed "war hawks" like Henry Clay and John C. Calhoun to push him into asking Congress to declare war in Britain. Although the war was initially unpopular, its satisfactory conclusion enhanced Madison's status, and he was increasingly admired after he left office in 1817.

In 1814, the end of the war in Europe enabled the British to send more troops to North America, and an amphibious operation in the Chesapeake in August took Washington, destroying the Capitol and the White House in revenge for the burning of York. The British bombardment of Baltimore provided Francis Scott Key with the words for "The Star Spangled Banner". Peace negotiations began at Ghent in August 1814, but as they dragged on, the British mounted a major offensive in the south. Edward Pakenham, Wellington's brother-in-law, was defeated and killed by Andrew Jackson's men at New Orleans in January 1815. Although the news had not reached North America, the Treaty of Ghent had been concluded, bringing a return to the status quo. Napoleon had helped bring the war about, but it had little effect in diverting the British from theatres they regarded as more important.

Edward Pakenham (1778–1815)

Pakenham was, like Wellington – who became his brother-in-law – the younger son of an Irish peer. He commanded the 64th Foot in the West Indies, went to the Peninsula in 1809, heading a brigade and a division, and earned particular approbation for handling the 3rd Division at Salamanca in 1812. Arriving in Louisiana in December 1814, he found his army in a very poor position, and failed in an ill-coordinated attack on the Americans south of New Orleans. He was killed trying to rally his men: his last words were said to be: "Lost for the lack of courage."

CHAPTER TWENTY-TWO

RUSSIA:

THE NIEMEN TO

MOSCOW

**In 1812 Napoleon launched against
Russia the largest army ever seen, but the
ultimate failure of this, his most ambitious
strike, would undermine the very
foundations of the Empire.**

Napoleon had relished the meetings at Tilsit in 1807, with the King of Prussia at his mercy and Tsar Alexander under his spell. Alexander implemented the Continental System, despite its cost to Russian commerce. Napoleon in turn refrained from offending him by making his creation the Grand Duchy of Warsaw into the Kingdom of Poland, and he even proposed a joint expedition to India. The meeting between the two sovereigns at Erfurt 1808 seemed cordial, and when a French actor declaimed "The friendship of a great man is a gift of the gods," Alexander ostentatiously shook Napoleon's hand. However, the tsar assured his patriotic mother that this was show: he would fight when he was ready.

The breach was gradual. In November 1810, Napoleon's foreign minister de Champagny warned him that "a vast revolution" against French control of Germany was imminent, and Napoleon was sure that Russian agents were fomenting it. Napoleon's betrothal to the Austrian princess Marie-Louise affronted the tsar, for he had been discussing a match between Napoleon and his younger sister. Although there was no new Kingdom of Poland, there was anger in Russia over the creation of the Grand Duchy, and a powerful undercurrent of nationalism, strengthened by the humiliations of Austerlitz and Friedland. When, in 1810, Bernadotte – a French Marshal – was elected Crown Prince of Sweden (which ruled Pomerania, on the south coast of the Baltic) mistrust of France deepened. Although Bernadotte was in fact to behave as an independent monarch and not a French puppet, it all seemed like nepotism. In August 1811, Napoleon told the Russian ambassador that he suspected Alexander of intending to invade the Grand Duchy, and by January 1812 both sides were preparing for war.

Mikhail Bogdanovich, Prince Barclay de Tolly (1761–1818)

Barclay was a scion of a Baltic family of Scots descent. Commissioned after long service in the ranks, he fought the Swedes and the Poles before distinguishing himself in the 1806–07 campaign against Napoleon, earning promotion to Lieutenant-General. In 1812 he combined the posts of Commander in Chief of the western armies and Minister of War, and although replaced in the former role by Kutusov he led his own army with marked skill at Borodino. He was Commander in Chief again for the campaigns of 1813–15. His "foreign" descent and Russian preference for characters like Suvorov (tenacious, brave, coarse and brutal) told against him: he was a good general and an important reformer.

The Russian army had been remodelled by War Minister Barclay de Tolly, and numbered over 400,000 men, part now organized into corps. Although officers were still poorly trained and staff procedures were cumbersome, there were some promising generals, notably Barclay himself and Prince Bagration. Prince Kutusov, who took command during the campaign, was past his best, but his courage, experience and abiding Russianness made him popular with the rank and file. Napoleon assembled the largest force history had seen. There were some 500,000 men in three first-line armies, and two auxiliary armies (80,000 under Eugène and 70,000 under Jerome Bonaparte), with a further 32,500 men on the Baltic coast and 34,000 Austrians on the right flank. There were 165,000 men in second-line formations, with a reserve of 60,000 in Germany and the Grand Duchy, and 10,000 Danes in Holstein. Fewer than half the first- and second-line troops were French, and, for all Napoleon's colossal energy and painstaking preparations, controlling a force of this size was beyond his means.

Prince Petr Ivanovich Bagration (1765–1812)

Bagration sprang from a noble Georgian family and joined the Russian army in 1782. He fought in Poland before serving in Italy and Switzerland in 1799. In subsequent campaigns he emerged as a tenacious rearguard commander, and his blazing courage illuminated a bleak day at Friedland. In 1808, he led a march across the frozen Gulf of Bothnia to capture the Aaland islands. He was mortally wounded commanding the left wing at Borodino. The Russian offensive which recaptured Belarus in 1944 was, fittingly, codenamed Operation Bagration.

Napoleon proposed to strike eastwards, while Jerome, on his right, folded back towards Warsaw, drawing the Russians after him, allowing Napoleon to pivot southwards for a battle of encirclement around Grodno. The Russians deployed two field armies, Barclay's first and Bagration's second, with a third army under Tormassov forming up behind them.

The French crossed the Niemen river on 23 June, but found that the Russians did not behave as expected. Pouring rain and poor roads slowed movement, and none of the planned encirclements worked. The well-conceived "manoeuvre of Smolensk" led to a battle on 17 August, and, although the French took the city, they failed to trap Barclay.

We cannot say if the Russian withdrawal was deliberately planned, and a growing sense of dissatisfaction at retreat encouraged Alexander to place Kutusov in command. He took up a position near the village of Borodino, 120km (75 miles) from Moscow, on the Kalatsha, a tributary of the Moskva, and strengthened it with field fortifications. Napoleon attacked him there on 7 September. Although the French stormed the main Russian defence at the Great Redoubt, the Russians fought with their customary stubbornness. By the end of that shocking day, the French had lost at least 30,000 men and the Russians perhaps 44,000 – about one in three of the combatants. The French entered Moscow on 14 September. There had still been no decisive battle, and it was already late in the year.

CHAPTER TWENTY-THREE

RUSSIA:

FIRE & SNOW

**Moscow was undefended: many
inhabitants had fled, and the remainder
refused to acknowledge the French.**

It was not long before hungry soldiers broke into shuttered houses and
shops. Worse was to come. The city's governor, Count Rostopchin, had
prepared to burn warehouses containing anything that might be useful
to the invaders, and ordered the evacuation of the city's fire-engines.
His men began the arson, but it was continued by criminals intent on
theft, and on 15 September, a strong wind spread the flames through the
timber-built city. Looting became widespread, and discipline broke down
as the polyglot horde of the *Grande Armée* robbed and raped. Things
were so bad that Napoleon left the city, and he returned to Moscow
on 18 September to find two-thirds of it burned. He sent messages to
Alexander, telling one emissary "I want peace, I need peace, I must have
peace," but did not understand that in burning their capital the Russians

had given an unmistakable sign that this was war to the knife. The messenger who carried news of Moscow's fall to Alexander reassured his sovereign: "The entry of the enemy into Moscow is not the conquest of Russia."

The French line of communication was clogged by wounded from Borodino and by surly reinforcements, often procured by scraping the barrel of allied manpower. Things were not much better for the Russians, with squabbling amongst senior officers and looting by stragglers and Cossacks. There was no guarantee that the Russian autocracy would survive the shock of Moscow's fall. Many Russians began to hedge their bets in case the regime collapsed, and serfs, sometimes emboldened by success as impromptu guerrillas, refused to obey their masters. But – not for the last time in Russian history – invasion conjured up a passion which sprang as much from popular enthusiasm as governmental encouragement.

Michel Ney (1769–1815)

Ney, a cooper's son from Sarrelouis, joined the hussars in 1787. Commissioned with the Revolution, he became a general in 1796 after abundant campaigning, and was made Marshal in 1804. A successful corps commander from 1805–07, he clashed with Masséna in Spain and was sent home in 1811. In 1812 he commanded the rearguard with superb courage (becoming Prince of the Moscowa), but was never the same afterwards. He rallied to Napoleon in 1815 and led haphazard attacks at Waterloo. Tried by his peers, he was shot against the wall of the Luxembourg Gardens: he himself gave the order to fire.

Alexander soon declared that he would not negotiate, and is reputed to have said: "This is the moment when my campaign begins." Already, on 24 September, a party of Napoleon's Guard cavalry had been destroyed trying to reopen the main road at Mojaisk, and pressure on the line of communication, 580km (360 miles) wide at its base and running 900km (550 miles) to Moscow, was stepped up. On 18 October, Napoleon decided to retreat on Kaluga, coinciding with Kutusov's decision to advance. On 24–25 October, there was a sharp battle for the bridge over the Luzha just north of Maloyaroslavets, and this persuaded Napoleon, who could still have used that route and retained some initiative, to move back onto the road along which he had advanced into Russia.

The retreat took the French past Borodino with its wolf-gnawed corpses. Napoleon was at Viazma on 31 October, and received news that while Kutusov was pressing his rearguard, a second Russian force under Tshitshagov was around Brest-Litovsk, ready to fall on his southern flank, and another, under Wittgenstein, was putting pressure on the north. Order had broken down in many regiments before the first snow fell on 3 November, and when the army reached Smolensk a week later it found few of the hoped-for supplies. On 17 November, Napoleon used the Guard, whose morale was holding up well, to clear the route by a sharp counter-attack at Krasnoe. Ney, whose corps had become separated from the main army, rejoined it on 21 November, to general rejoicing.

When the French reached the River Berezina they found its bridges destroyed and water flowing freely after a sudden thaw. However, discovery of a ford north of Borisov enabled troops to cross to protect the engineers as they constructed trestle bridges, and feints up and down the river persuaded Tshitshagov to overlook the real crossing in favour of a diversion. The survivors crossed on 25–29 November, and lurched on westwards, the indomitable Ney commanding the rearguard. On 5 December, Napoleon handed over command to Murat, and departed post-haste for Paris. He had probably lost 400,000 French and allied soldiers. One historian puts losses on both sides, military and civilian, at two million. Casualties on this scale made the campaign more costly in human life than, say, the 1916 battles of the Somme and Verdun combined. It was a catastrophe from which Napoleon was never fully to recover.

CHAPTER TWENTY-FOUR

MILITARY

MEDICINE

**It may be a cliché to say that wounds and
death are the currency of war, but the
Napoleonic era saw this coinage paid out in
unprecedented amounts.**

Napoleon once asked a Russian negotiator: "Has your master, like me,
25,000 men a month to spend?" Advances in medical science such
as the discovery of ether and chloroform were still up to half a century
away. The best a man on the surgeon's bench could hope for was a swig
of alcohol, and a leather strap to bite as the knife went in. Hygiene and
sanitation were poorly understood, and disease killed more soldiers than
cannon, musket or sabre. The British army in the Peninsula lost 8,889
men to enemy fire and 24,900 to sickness, the French expeditionary
force sent to Santo Domingo lost over 20,000 officers and men to yellow
fever in a few months, and there were 50,000 French sick and wounded

in Spain in December 1808. Even the comparatively salubrious Leghorn saw an epidemic which carried off 800 men of the 62nd of the Line.

Soldiers actually killed in battle were outnumbered by those who

James McGrigor (1771–1858)

McGrigor joined the 88th Foot as its surgeon in 1793 without having completed his degree, in itself an index of the state of British military medicine. A humane man whose first night in an officers' mess gave him a lifelong hatred of heavy drinking, McGrigor served in the colonies and Flanders before becoming Wellington's senior medical officer in the Peninsula. He established small regimental hospitals which offered prompt treatment, and did his best to ensure that larger hospitals were properly run. After the war he was director-general of the army's medical department, and did much to improve the status and professional competence of medical officers. In 1850 they were made eligible for the Order of the Bath: the *Lancet* called it "the greatest step ever made by our profession towards obtaining its just recognition by the state". Wellington called him "one of the most industrious, able and successful public servants I have ever met". It was a measure of his success that he was given a baronetcy and made a Knight Commander of the Bath.

died afterwards from the effects of their wounds. Men with penetrating wounds of the abdomen were far more likely to die than live, even if they received prompt treatment. A musket ball often carried unburned powder, wadding and soiled clothing into the wound, and infection was almost inevitable. If a man survived the shock or haemorrhage caused by amputation – the common treatment for limbs damaged by musketry or cannon-fire – he was still likely to perish from post-operative infection.

At the beginning of the period the French army had a doctor for each battalion, and maintained both field and static hospitals. Larrey, who had served with Napoleon in Italy and Egypt, was a skilled organizer and natural improviser who recognized the need to get wounded soldiers from the battlefield to field hospitals as quickly as possible. He designed two kinds of sprung carriage, a light, two-wheeled version which could carry two stretcher cases, and a four-wheeled version which took four men. His first "flying ambulance" was the model for larger units, each "a legion of 340, comprising officers, NCOs and privates" which could be split up into three divisions, with 12 light and four heavy carriages each, or kept together as the situation demanded. His colleague Percy shared the desire to bring aid to the wounded as swiftly as possible, but preferred to use an ambulance wagon to get surgeons forward, and developed the use of stretcher-bearers to collect the wounded and carry them in to an aid post. Larrey's system became standard in Napoleon's armies, though Percy's stretcher-bearers were also adopted.

Larrey believed in operating promptly, certainly within 24 hours, and

---

Dominique Jean Larrey (1766–1842)

Larrey, the son of poor parents, was trained by his surgeon uncle in Toulouse. He went on to Paris, where he became a naval surgeon after a brilliant examination performance. Seasickness forced him ashore, and he held a series of appointments under Napoleon, rising to become medical Inspector-General in 1805. He served in all major campaigns, and was made a baron after Wagram. Although he followed Napoleon (who bequeathed him 100,000 francs) in the Hundred Days, he was lauded by the Bourbons, and widely respected for his skill, humanity and humour.

---

ideally as soon as possible after the wound was incurred. He personally conducted some 200 amputations during and immediately after the battle of Borodino. Unusually for the surgeons of his day, he understood the danger of premature closure of a wound, and his emphasis on *débridement* – the removal of non-living tissue from the wound – has been revived from time to time, most recently by British surgeons in the Falklands in 1982. Percy was more cautious about amputation, but when it was necessary he believed that speed was essential, and eight seconds was his target time for removing a limb.

Medical services were always swamped by major battles, and Borodino – its carnage not equalled till the first day of the Somme in 1916 – left French and Russian wounded strewn about an inhospitable landscape. Many of the French were crammed into the monastery at Kolotskoie and distributed around various buildings in Mozhaisk, but the official responsible for them had no medical equipment and no nurses: many of his charges died of hunger and thirst. The French, like most armies of the day, placed their doctors under the control of the army's administrative services, run by civilian officials, and although doctors had officer status they lacked the formal authority of commissioned officers. It would take more wars and more suffering for medical services to be thoroughly reformed.

CHAPTER TWENTY-FIVE

THE SPANISH ULCER 1812 - 14

Early in 1812, Wellington fell on Ciudad Rodrigo, the northernmost of the two fortresses that guarded the Spanish frontier, storming it on 19 January.

He then moved south to Badajoz, a much more strongly fortified position, wedged between the Guadiana river and the Rivallas brook and garrisoned by 4,000 French soldiers. The siege began on 17 March, and on the night of 6 April, the British mounted a general assault, eventually forcing their way in with heavy loss. The attackers, maddened by the sights they had seen and the drink they stole, behaved appallingly, and Wellington was so furious that he could scarcely bring himself to thank them.

There were still over 230,000 French soldiers in Spain, and Wellington had only 70,000 British and Portuguese regulars. But the

French, split up between five armies whose commanders often did not see eye-to-eye, had to cope with Spanish regulars and guerrillas as well as Wellington, and were unable to concentrate against him. Wellington debated whether to strike against Soult in the south or at Marmont in the north but eventually, having destroyed the Tagus bridge at Almaraz to prevent them from supporting one another, decided to deal with Marmont. He reached Salamanca in mid-June, and on 22 July, after much marching and counter-marching, noticed that Marmont's army was strung out along its line of march. He launched an attack which left the French army reeling backwards: had the Spanish garrison not withdrawn from the bridge at Alba de Tormes, it is likely that not a man would have escaped.

Robert Craufurd (1764–1812)

Craufurd, the third son of a Scots baronet, commanded the 75th Foot in the Mysore War of 1790–92, but is best known for commanding the Light Brigade (later the Light Division) in the Peninsula. Craufurd was foul-tempered and rash: he was lucky to get away with engaging Ney on the Coa in 1810. But although he was a harsh disciplinarian, a rifleman said: "I do not think I ever admired a man who wore the British uniform more than I did General Craufurd." He was mortally wounded at the storming of Ciudad Rodrigo.

There was now nothing to stop Wellington taking Madrid, and he entered the Spanish capital on 12 August. But he mishandled his next move, botched the siege of Burgos – recently refortified on Napoleon's orders – and on 21 October, retreated towards Portugal with the French in hot pursuit. He went into winter quarters just across the Portuguese border while the survivors of the *Grande Armée* reeled back from Russia. In the spring of 1813, there were still 200,000 Frenchmen in Spain, but no prospect of their being reinforced, and Wellington's excellent intelligence service told him that Joseph and Victor, with the main enemy army, more than 66,000 strong, had abandoned Madrid and were trying to join Clausel in the north-west. Joseph's army was encumbered with all the trappings of his court (one general called it "a walking bordello") and Wellington's 80,000 men caught it at Vitoria in the valley of the River Zadorra on 28 June. The din of his victory echoed across Europe: a Te Deum was sung in St Petersburg, and Beethoven composed *Wellington's Victory* in its honour.

August Fréderic Louis Viesse de Marmont (1774–1852)

Marmont was an artillery officer in the royal army who did well after accepting the Revolution. He helped Napoleon with the Brumaire coup, and was vexed not to be made Marshal in the 1804 creation. He implemented Napoleon's artillery reforms and was a successful field commander, receiving his marshal's baton in 1809. Wellington beat him at Salamanca, and in 1814 his early surrender coined a play on his title – Duke of Ragusa – so that *"raguser"* came to mean to betray. Yet he stayed loyal to the Bourbon Charles X, following him into exile in 1830.

Soult took command of the French armies on the Pyrenees, and restored morale before mauling British detachments at Roncesvalles and Maya. Wellington checked him at Sorauren, and went on to storm San Sebastián in September. Having forced the crossing of the Bidossoa, Wellington unravelled Soult's defence on French soil in the battles of the Nivelle, the Nive and St Pierre, and went on to threaten Bayonne. He beat Soult at Orthez on 27 February 1814, but still needed to be cautious in case Suchet slipped north from Catalonia to join Soult. In April, he attacked Soult around Toulouse, but the French slipped away after a well-handled defence. On 12 April, Wellington was dressing for dinner in the city when a galloper arrived with news that Napoleon had abdicated on 6 April.

CHAPTER TWENTY-SIX

THE HOME FRONT: NAPOLEONIC FRANCE

If Napoleon's legal, educational and administrative reforms left an enduring mark on France, the physical symbols of Empire were scarcely less striking.

After Napoleon's coronation, suggested one contemporary: "The revival of old customs gave occupation to tradespeople who could get no employment under the Directory or Consulate, such as saddlers, carriagemakers, lacemen, embroiderers and others. By these positive interests were created more partisans of the Empire than by opinions and reflections." The period christened its own decorative and architectural style, with classical form and ornament, rich ormolu, ebony and hardstone, scattered with imperial eagles and Bonaparte bees. There was a self-conscious recognition that these were great days. When David's huge painting of the coronation was displayed in 1808, Boilly painted the crowd that had come to see it: art was imitating itself.

Napoleon established "grand imperial dignitaries" for his court, and created an imperial nobility, finding dukes, counts and barons from amongst soldiers, administrators, scientists, artists and professional men. If there was something slightly tawdry about the process (some old nobility would have nothing to do with it, while others found themselves strangely attracted to the new court), it bound the elite more closely to the regime, and offered the prospect of advancement to the humbly born. In 1809, Napoleon wished to reward the 13th Light Infantry, and asked its colonel to nominate the bravest man in the regiment. After consulting his officers, the colonel selected the drum major. "I appoint you a Knight of the Legion of Honour, Baron of the Empire, and award you a pension of 4,000 francs," declared the Emperor.

Napoleon had some success in developing the French economy, building on foundations established under the old regime and capitalizing on the brief peace following the Treaty of Amiens in 1802 to import British experts and techniques. Some of his public works, like the huge tunnel built to carry the St Quentin canal beneath a low ridge south of Cambrai, remain impressive. However, in general terms French industry lagged behind British: one estimate puts French industrialization in 1815 at the level of Britain in 1780. The Continental System did not help: France was excluded from overseas markets and denied imported

Joseph Fouché (1763–1820)

Fouché was elected to the Convention in 1792, voted for the king's execution, and went on to put down "counter-revolution" in Lyons with shocking severity. Made Minister of Police in 1799, he held the post, with interruptions, until 1815, and played a major part in ensuring the stability of Napoleon's rule (being rewarded with the title Duke of Otranto), through constantly intriguing with the Bourbons. He was responsible for instituting vigorous political censorship of books, plays and the press, and his ubiquitous network of spies and informers made him a man to be feared at every level of society. This thoroughly unscrupulous man's luck ran out in 1816 when he was exiled as a regicide.

raw materials. In 1808, the American consul at Bordeaux saw grass growing in the streets, and once-busy quays almost deserted. Attempts to compensate for absent raw materials had mixed success: chicory was grown as a substitute for coffee, and beet for sugar-cane.

There was a major industrial recession in 1811–12, which produced widespread unemployment and was accompanied by unusually poor harvests, pushing up grain and bread prices. March 1812 saw large-scale riots in Caen, put down with bloodshed, while in Rouen three ship-loads of rice, imported from England under special licence, as well as imports from Belgium (a historian has called this "the pillage economy of conquest") helped prevent an outbreak there. Imperial decrees which authorized requisitioning and fixed grain prices caused widespread resentment, and in many areas it seems that local efforts did as much as centralized authority to alleviate famine.

The most obvious symbol that France was at war was the constant pressure of conscription. Its burden varied. Only 30,000 men were required in 1801, and none the following year. But in 1803, 63,000 men were summoned from the classes of Years IX and X; in 1805 80,000 men were called up from that year's class, and another 100,000 reservists were mobilized. When Napoleon reached Paris in November 1813, he was told that by calling up both Frenchmen and selected allies he should be able to secure 500,000 men.

Conscription was determined by ballot. Even if he drew a bad number, a man could pay a replacement to serve on his behalf, and there were family and health exemptions, subject to manipulation at local level, where the draft was actually applied. There was a good deal of fraud, and, on a wider scale, *insoumission* (failure to attend the ballot or to report for training) and outright desertion. The system worked well enough, except when the Empire was visibly tottering. It was more successful in some regions than in others: Paris and the north-east were most compliant, and peasants were often better placed to evade the draft than townsmen. One official told his masters that public opinion was "totally contrary to conscription and the least recalcitrant are those who regard it as a necessary evil which is to be avoided ...". The refractory conscript, hiding out in the woods, haunted public imagination and affronted imperial authority.

CHAPTER TWENTY-SEVEN

THE BATTLE OF THE NATIONS

Whatever imperial bulletins might say, the scale of Napoleon's catastrophe in Russia was obvious, and the coalition against him gained strength.

In April 1812, the tsar had made an agreement of mutual assistance with Bernadotte, now Regent of Sweden. Britain endorsed the arrangement at the Treaty of Stockholm in March 1813, and Prussia, whose army had already ceased co-operation with the French, acceded to it the following month. In May 1812, the Treaty of Bucharest had ended Russo-Turkish hostilities, leaving Russia free to concentrate on her major enemy. Austria was still a French ally, but the supple Metternich, her foreign minister, could sense the political current, and eventually, after much agonizing diplomacy in the summer and autumn of 1813, the Convention of Teplitz at last brought Austria into the coalition. The whole arrangement was underpinned by huge British subsidies: what Napoleon had disdainfully called a nation of shopkeepers was paymaster to the coalition that would bring him down.

The year 1813 began badly for the French. Eugène de Beauharnais, left facing the Russians and, after Prussia's formal reversal of allegiance, vengeful Prussians too, fell back steadily, abandoning both Frankfurt-on-Oder and Dresden. In mid-April, Napoleon moved up to Mainz, intent on a major counter-offensive, though his weakness in cavalry following the large-scale loss of horses in Russia caused him great concern. On the morning of 2 May, Marmont and Ney came close to being swamped at Lützen, but in the afternoon Napoleon recovered the situation with a deft counter-attack which left the allies badly rattled. There was another hard-fought battle at Bautzen on 20–21 May, when Ney's unthinking determination in launching repeated assaults on the village of Preititz instead of circumventing it, and lack of cavalry deprived Napoleon of what might have been a major victory. However, it jolted allied confidence, and the Russians and Prussians fell back into Silesia to plan their next move. Austrian mediation persuaded both sides to accept an armistice, formally agreed at Plaswitz on 4 June.

The armistice was extended into August while the opponents negotiated with one another and the allies sought – eventually with success – to bring Austria into their camp. When the campaign reopened, Napoleon, who had used the lull to bring his army up to almost 400,000 men, made several short-lived attempts to fall on isolated allied contingents, and eventually decided to concentrate on Dresden, where

---

Jean Baptiste Jules Bernadotte (1763–1844)

Bernadotte joined the infantry in 1780 and was a sergeant-major by the Revolution. Promoted quickly, he married Napoleon's sister-in-law Desirée Clary, and was appointed Marshal in 1804. A patchy field commander, he was inactive at Auerstadt and was sacked at Wagram. But he behaved courteously to Swedish prisoners, and in 1810 was made Crown Prince – effectively Regent – of Sweden. Napoleon soon discovered that he was no puppet king, and in 1813–14 he fought against his former colleagues. He later observed: "I, who was once a Marshal of France, am now only King of Sweden."

Josef Anton, Prince Poniatowski (1763–1813)

Poniatowski was son of an Austrian general and nephew of a king of
Poland. Although he served in the Austrian army, and was wounded
fighting the Turks, he regarded himself as Polish. In 1789 the Polish
Assembly made him an army commander, and he fought the Russians
with unavailing distinction. When the Grand Duchy of Warsaw was
constituted in 1807 Napoleon offered him command of its army. He did
well in the 1809 campaign against Austria, but his corps was severely
depleted in 1812. Poniatowski, just appointed Marshal, was drowned
swimming the River Elster at the battle of Leipzig.

St-Cyr was facing attack by the allies. On 26 August, the attackers made
encouraging progress, but by nightfall most of their gains had been
swallowed up by French counter-attacks. The following day, French
assaults gained momentum, and allied commanders, bruised by the loss
of 38,000 men to perhaps 10,000 French, fell back that night. However,
injudicious pursuit in the face of a numerous enemy led to three separate
reverses in whose course the balance-sheet of Dresden was reversed.

Over the next weeks Napoleon twisted and turned, aware that his opponents were anxious to fight his subordinates but far less eager to try con-
clusions with him. Battle casualties, sickness and political fluctuation were
eroding his army. Bavaria had left his fold, and Germany seemed on the
verge of revolt. Napoleon decided to concentrate his army, though he left a
substantial force at Dresden. He first hoped to attack the two major allied
groupings separately, but by mid-October he knew that this was impossible:
the best that he could do would be to draw in and fight at Leipzig. The battle
saw him on the strategic defensive, but, characteristically, he planned to
use his agility to attack his heterogeneous enemies faster than they could
react. In a fierce four-day battle, fought by close to half a million men (the
world's largest military engagement until the First World War), sheer
weight of numbers and growing allied determination proved too much for
him. An error in blowing a bridge over the Elster left part of his army on
the wrong side, and in all perhaps 30,000 prisoners were added to 38,000
battle casualties. The allies lost over 50,000 men, but they could recover
from the carnage of this "Battle of the Nations". Napoleon could not.

CHAPTER TWENTY-EIGHT

NAPOLEON'S GREATEST ADVERSARIES

Napoleon's initial scorching successes encouraged adversaries who imitated his organization, though there were few who could match him.

When Napoleon was at the height of his powers, in Italy in 1796, or in 1805–06, there were few commanders who could touch him. But even he was beaten from time to time. Sometimes, as at Aspern-Essling in 1809, this was because he scorned his opponents and let self-confidence lead him into unjustifiable risks. In Russia in 1812 Napoleon made a strategic error on a grand scale, not simply underestimating the dogged fighting qualities of the Russian soldier (so well encapsulated in Kutusov), but misjudging both the character of the tsar and the impact of Russia's vast landscape on his army. And, after an impressive start to the campaign of the Hundred Days in 1815, he failed to ensure that Blücher's Prussians and Wellington's army were kept apart, and did not appreciate that breaking Wellington's position on the ridge of Mont St Jean would be a difficult business, not, as he snapped angrily to his staff, just a matter of "eating breakfast".

Gebhard von Blücher (1742–1819)

Blücher was an officer in Swedish service, but transferred his allegiance to the Prussian army after his capture by them in 1760. Having briefly left the army he was a lieutenant-general in 1802. He had a horse shot under him at Jena, and was subsequently forced to retire because of anti-French views. Reinstated and given command of the Army of Silesia in 1813, he was created Prince of Wahlstadt in 1814. In 1815 he commanded the Prussian army based on Liège, and, although beaten at Ligny, swung back to aid Wellington at Waterloo: without him there could have been no allied victory.

Even Napoleon's restless spirit was worn down by the burdens he imposed upon it. After 1805 he told his valet Constant that: "One only has a certain time for war. I will be good for six years more; after that even I must cry halt." By 1815, he was ill, with piles, bladder problems and disease of the pituitary gland amongst the candidates for causing his strangely withdrawn behaviour on the day of Waterloo. Napoleon was not always a sound judge of men. He forgave Bernadotte for failing to support Davout at Auerstadt in 1806, but then publicly dismissed him from command of his corps at Wagram. He privately described Ney as "brave and nothing more ... good at leading 10,000 men into battle, but other than that ... a real blockhead", yet gave him command of his left wing at Quatre Bras in 1815 and entrusted the major attack to him at Waterloo two days later.

But it is not enough to blame Napoleon's reverses on his own mistakes: the fact is that his opponents got better. One element of this improvement lay in the quickening pulse of nationalism that beat through Napoleonic Europe, and another in the imitation of French military success. For more than a decade after the Revolution France fought armies that were creatures of the age of Frederick the Great. Drill, discipline and turnout were all-important, and there was usually an uncrossable dividing line between officers and men. In 1796 a British officer attached to the Austrians in Italy saw how: "Some French sharpshooters, concealed by the bushes at the edge of the river ... kept up a very constant and annoying fire on the fine regiment of Kehl (three battalions) ... which were very absurdly drawn up on the top of a dyke forming the great road to the left bank of the river, occasionally making discharges to drive away their invisible enemies. By stepping back six or eight yards, and lying down on the reverse bank of the dyke, not a shot from the enemy would have told; whereas a loss of nearly 150 men was the consequence of this stupid bravado ..."

Charles, Archduke of Austria (1771–1847)

Charles was the third son of Leopold II. He had mixed success against the French in the Low Countries in 1792–93, and when commanding on the Rhine in 1796 beat Masséna and Jourdan, but saw his plans ruined by Moreau's victory at Hohenlinden (1800). As president of the Council of War he embarked upon wide-ranging reform, a process which continued after Austerlitz. He beat Napoleon at Essling in 1809, but lost at Wagram two months later. He received no significant military employment thereafter, and it took the efforts of his son Albrecht, himself a distinguished general, to gain him historical recognition.

Military initiative and national sentiment were alike discouraged. After Jena in 1806, the Prussian government announced that: "The king has lost a battle. Calm is the duty of every citizen."

By 1813, nothing could have been more different. King Frederick William's proclamation *An Mein Volk* was enthusiastically received, and there were volunteers for the Prussian army across Germany: the coming campaign was known as "The War of Liberation". In February,

Mikhail Ilarionovich Golenischev-Kutusov (1745–1813)

Kutusov, the son of a military engineer, campaigned in Poland in 1764–69 and against the Turks in 1770–74, losing an eye. A major-general in 1784, he fought the Turks again in 1787–92. In 1805, he led the first Russian army sent to Austria and won a victory at Dürrenstein. He argued against attacking at Austerlitz, where he was wounded. Fresh from a campaign on the Danube against the Turks, he took command in August 1812, fought Napoleon at Borodino, and pursued him from Russia, gaining the title Prince of Smolensk. Often depicted as a wily old peasant, Kutusov was urbane and intelligent, though with a powerful appetite for girls and drink.

Prussia accepted the principle of universal military service, organizing volunteer *jäger* detachments and a *Landwehr* for men not required for the regular army, and appointing officers from a range of social backgrounds. The inhabitants of some other German states had never wholly accepted French occupation. The King's German Legion, largely recruited from inhabitants of Hanover (also ruled by Britain's George III) constituted one of the best elements of Wellington's army in the Peninsula and at Waterloo, and two successive Dukes of Brunswick died fighting the French. Although things were not the same in Austria, where tensions between the different nationalities never abated, there were still attempts to replace old-fashioned discipline with a sense of national purpose and self-value. "Love of his monarch and an honest life," announced the *Infantry Regulations of 1807*, part of the Archduke Charles's reforms, "obedience, loyalty, resolution, these are the soldierly virtues. In one word, a soldier must be a nobleman." Both Prussia and Austria instituted awards, the Iron Cross for the former and the Army Cross for the latter, that were available to all ranks.

Napoleon's opponents paid attention to his military organization. The corps system was widely imitated: even the Duke of Wellington, a born centralizer, had his British and Dutch-Belgian army divided into three corps for the Hundred Days. Skirmishers were more widely used. The Austrians did their best to develop skirmishing, but remained too formal about it, leading Radetzky, arguably the best Austrian general to

Arthur Wellesley (1769–1852)

Wellesley, the third surviving son of an Irish peer, was commissioned into the infantry in 1787. He fought in the Low Countries in 1793–94 and then went to India, rising to Major-General and beating the Mahrattas at Assaye in 1803. After a succession of military and civil appointments he was sent to French-occupied Portugal in 1808, winning Vimeiro but narrowly escaping disgrace over the terms of the Convention of Cintra, which the British government thought had let off the defeated French too lightly. Sent back to the Peninsula in 1809, he won a series of victories, beginning with Talavera, which led to his being made Viscount Wellington. Successive victories brought him a dukedom. In 1815 he commanded the army based around Brussels, and worked closely with Blücher to win Waterloo. He later went into politics, serving as Prime Minister in 1828–30.

emerge from the wars, to complain: "operations *en tirailleure* can only be conducted in a very limited manner because we do not understand this kind of fighting." It was remarkable how the British, initially mistrustful of light troops, developed both green-jacketed infantrymen and red-coated light infantry, paying French skirmishers back in their own leaden coin. It remained true that few opponents could stand before the Emperor at his best: but the balance of advantage tilted steadily against him.

Karl Wilhelm Ferdinand, Duke of Brunswick (1735–1806)

Brunswick made his reputation in Prussian service in the Seven Years' War, and commanded Austrian and Prussian forces in the War of the First Coalition, but declined to force an issue against the French at Valmy in 1792. He was mortally wounded at Auerstadt in 1806. His son Friedrich Wilhelm (1771–1815) fled to England in 1806 and led his "Black Brunswickers" in the Peninsula and the campaign of the Hundred Days. He was killed at Quatre Bras.

CHAPTER TWENTY-NINE

THE

CHAMPAGNE

CAMPAIGN

**In early 1814, the allies, heartened by
victory at Leipzig, approached the natural
frontiers of France.**

Blücher's Prussians crossed the Meuse in late January, and Schwarzenberg's Austrians advanced on the Langres plateau. The danger of these two forces joining and then moving on Paris encouraged Napoleon to take the field in person, and he arrived at Châlons on 26 January, hoping to use the area's good road system to allow him to strike at his opponents in turn.

Napoleon first tried to catch Blücher at Brienne, where he had attended military school as a young man, but a crucial order was intercepted by Cossacks and the battle was more evenly balanced than he had hoped. French infantry, young conscripts for the most part, fought surprisingly well, and forced their way into the chateau: Blücher pulled back after a desperate attempt to retake it. Napoleon, with some 40,000 men, followed the retreating Prussians and redeployed other forces to cover his flanks. As he did so, Schwarzenberg joined Blücher at Trannes, south-west of La Rothière, and advanced to meet Napoleon with over 50,000 men, with more close behind. The battle of La Rothière was fought in a snow-storm on 1 February. It see-sawed both ways, but eventually Barclay's Russians came up, and Napoleon had to break contact in the darkness, having lost 6,000 men and 50 guns in the battle and losing another 4,000 deserters by the time he reached Troyes.

Karl Philip, Prince Schwarzenberg (1771–1820)

Schwarzenberg joined the Austrian army in 1787 and saved the right wing of the defeated army at Hohenlinden. He got a division out of the trap at Ulm, and fought at Wagram. Schwarzenberg handled negotiations for the marriage of Marie-Louise, and Napoleon asked for him to command the Austrian contingent in 1812. Promoted Field Marshal, he commanded the coalition army which lost at Dresden but won at Leipzig, complaining that he was beset by "fools of every description, eccentric project makers, intriguers, asses, babblers ...". He beat Napoleon at Arcis-sur-Aube and La Fère-Champenoise in 1814.

In the days that followed, Schwarzenberg proceeded with character-istic caution, while Blücher struck out confidently for Paris, weakening the link between them. Showing a dazzling flash of his old form, Napoleon decided to hook north to deal with the Prussians, leaving Mortier to persuade the cautious Schwarzenberg to fall back on Bar-sur-Aube, and collecting a newly formed corps under Oudinot so that he stood – now with 70,000 men – between the main allied forces. His cavalry reported that Blücher was heading towards Paris via Champaubert and Montmirail. He first detached Victor and Oudinot to watch Schwarzenberg, before wholly outmanoeuvring his opponents, destroying one Russian corps at Champaubert on 10 February, mauling another at Montmirail and punishing a Prussian corps too. Before moving south to deal with Schwarzenberg, now on the move again, Napoleon found time to give Blücher a drubbing at Vauchamps. He then hurtled down on Schwarzenberg, demolishing outlying columns on 17 February and shoving Württemberg's corps back through Montereau on 18 February.

Edouard Adolphe Casimir Mortier (1768–1835)

Mortier was a bourgeois from Le Câteau in northern France, who was elected a National Guard captain in 1791 and was a brigadier in 1799. His conquest of Hanover in 1803 earned him appointment as Marshal the following year, and he was made Duke of Treviso in 1808. Mortier was a dogged corps commander, and was designated to command the Old Guard in 1815 had he not been ill. Having survived a dozen major battles, he died in a Paris street when an "infernal machine" intended for King Louis-Philippe hit him instead.

These defeats persuaded the allied leaders to reconsider their strategy, but they undertook to fight on with no separate treaties, offering Napoleon peace on the basis of the frontiers of 1791, which he immediately rejected. He then turned north to cross the Aisne and attack Blücher in an inconclusive battle at Craonne, before biting off more than he could chew on 9–10 March at Laon, losing 6,000 men that he could ill afford. He partly retrieved his situation by retaking Rheims and capturing its defenders, and then jinked back to face Schwarzenberg yet again, only to run into the entire enemy army at Arcis-sur-Aube. He managed to get across the river and break clear, and then, aggressive to the last, decided to head for St-Mihiel in the hope of ravaging allied communications.

But the game was up. French dispatches were routinely captured, enabling the allies to stake all on an advance on Paris, whose morale was palpably wavering. Napoleon was decoyed into attacking the Russian commander Winzingerode on 26 March, and by the time he heard that the allies had beaten Mortier and Marmont at La Fère Champenoise it was too late to get back to cover the capital. He collected all the troops he could at Fontainebleau, where Ney, the generals' spokesman, told him that the army would not march on Paris. News that Marmont had gone over to the allies persuaded him to abdicate in favour of his son, but the allies demanded unconditional abdication, which Napoleon duly signed on 6 April. On 12 April, he decided to kill himself, and took the mixture of opium, belladonna and white hellebore which he had carried in a sachet round his neck since his narrow escape from the Russians in 1812. The poison's efficacy had diminished over the years, and he soon recovered. The Treaty of Fontainebleau, its final form agreed on 16 April, allowed Napoleon to retain his imperial title, and gave him sovereignty over the island of Elba with two million francs a year and a guard of 600 men. He was taken there, fittingly, by a British warship, leaving France on 29 May, the very day that Josephine died of pneumonia at Malmaison.

CHAPTER THIRTY

THE CONGRESS

OF VIENNA

**At Vienna, the allies met in a fractious
Congress to divide up the spoils of Napoleon's
defeat, but the Emperor's return rendered its
few achievements superfluous.**

In one sense, Napoleon's abdication changed nothing, for Louis XVIII, younger brother of the executed Louis XVI, had become titular king on the death of the Dauphin, unlucky child of Louis XVI and Marie-Antoinette, in 1795. On 12 April 1814, his brother the Comte d'Artois, acting as the king's lieutenant-general, entered an enthusiastic Paris and heard a Te Deum in Notre Dame. Louis, who had been living in England, followed more slowly, arriving at Boulogne on 24 April, and reaching the capital on 3 May. He had already promised France representative government, individual liberty, freedom of the press and an independent judiciary. Perhaps more to the point, he had agreed to recognize the sales of national property carried out by previous regimes, and acknowledged imperial ranks, titles, pensions and debts.

It was soon clear that the Bourbons had "learned nothing and forgotten nothing". There was no firm government, because that would have meant a chief minister. Many Napoleonic veterans were compulsorily retired from the army, and émigrés appointed in their place. The old Royal Guard was recreated, and the Bourbon flag replaced the tricoleur. Philippe de Ségur, a nobleman of the old regime who had served with distinction under Napoleon, complained that: "They imposed on us the flag under which they had fought us." And Count Maximilien Foy lamented: "We who were lately masters of Europe, to what servitude are we reduced? ... O Napoleon, where are you?"

Klemens Wenzel Nepomuk Lothar, Prince Metternich (1773–1859)

Metternich was one of the most powerful reactionary influences of his age. He studied at Strasbourg and Mainz before holding a number of diplomatic posts, and became Foreign Minister of Austria in 1809. He negotiated the marriage between Napoleon and Marie-Louise, played a prominent part in the Congress of Vienna, and dominated the Empire's politics with rigid conservatism until 1848, when the government's collapse in that "year of revolutions" saw him flee to Britain. In 1851, he retired to his castle of Johannesberg on the Rhine.

While disillusionment spread in France, the great powers – Austria, Britain, France, Prussia and Russia – met at Vienna in September 1814 to reorder their world. Their aim was not to punish France for past misdeeds, but to construct a Europe which would not tolerate the rise of a new Napoleon. Castlereagh, the British foreign secretary, declared that he was there "not to collect trophies but to bring the world back to peaceful habits". Yet if it had been hard to hold an alliance together in the face of a threat from Napoleon, with that threat now removed it was difficult indeed to make progress. Wellington had been British ambassador in Paris, where he had bought Pauline Borghese's wonderful mansion in the rue du Faubourg St Honoré, which still houses the British embassy, and he was dispatched to Vienna in early 1815. He knew that prospects were poor, having been told by Castlereagh that: "I send you ... the result of our discussions, not progress; for progress we have not made." However, if debate had produced no results, there were a good deal of balls, banquets and hunting parties, and the old Prince de Ligne quipped "*Le congrès ne marche pas, mais il danse*," loosely translated as "The Congress does not work, but it plays."

Alexander I, Tsar of Russia (1777–1825)

Alexander succeeded his murdered father Paul in 1801 and began his reign as an enthusiastic reformer. He joined the coalition against Napoleon in 1805, but had to make peace at Tilsit in 1807, and fell briefly under Napoleon's spell. After the French invasion in 1812 he pursued the war resolutely, and, at the Congress of Vienna when Napoleon escaped from Elba, urged its vigorous resumption. He was the moving spirit behind the Holy Alliance, and his later years were dominated by conservatism and mysticism. Some believed that he did not die in 1825 but assumed the identity of the hermit Feodor Kuzmich.

Tsar Alexander, jolted heavily towards religious romanticism by the events of 1812, favoured a "Sacred League" or "Holy Alliance", an attempt to base world peace on a Europe united by Christian principles. It was, though, important that these principles had a Russian flavour: Alexander hoped to swallow the whole of Poland, compensating Prussia for losses there by giving her Saxony, and hoping that Austria would recoup her own lost Polish territory by gains in north Italy.

Castlereagh thought that discussions might end in a new war, or at best in slow progress, and believed it useful for Britain and France to work closely and to try to attract Austria. However, Talleyrand, the arch-intriguer who had been Napoleon's foreign minister and now served the Bourbons, got on badly with Castlereagh. Wellington, still in Paris, was able to get Louis to order him to be more co-operative, and a secret treaty was signed between Britain, France and Austria in January 1815. The tsar was persuaded to content himself with the former Grand Duchy of Warsaw rather than the whole of Poland, and total breakdown seemed less likely.

When Wellington arrived in February 1815 he asked what had been achieved. Metternich, the Austrian foreign minister, replied: "Nothing; absolutely nothing." Wellington knew that, in the persons of Metternich and Talleyrand, he was dealing with two remarkably devious statesmen, and hoped "to go straight forward without stratagems or subterfuges". He was helped by the fact that the tsar held him in high regard, and although he complained that the overheated rooms "have almost killed me", it seemed as if the Congress might produce useful results after all. Then, on 7 March, came the startling news that Napoleon had escaped from Elba. Nobody was sure where he would go, but the majority thought Italy most probable: how wrong they were.

CHAPTER THIRTY-ONE

THE 100 DAYS:

RETURN

& ATTACK

**Napoleon's new kingdom-in-exile on Elba
had a population of just 13,700, and his
"palace", a former mill, only a dozen rooms.**

He became bored and, apparently, increasingly withdrawn, but remained in contact with his supporters in France, and in February 1815 he decided to escape, taking with him the 600 men of his Guard and four cannon. His customary good luck held, and he avoided British and French warships to land near Cannes on 1 March. So began the Hundred Days of his restoration.

Local authorities were taken by surprise, and Napoleon set off by a mountainous route which would take him to Lyons. He first real test came at Laffrey, 25km (15 miles) south of Grenoble, where a regiment turned out to stop him. "If there is any one amongst you who wishes to kill his Emperor, here I am," said Napoleon, throwing open his coat:

soon hundreds of men were yelling *"Vive l'Empereur"*. Grenoble opened its gates, and on 10 March he entered Lyons without resistance. As he moved on, haranguing crowds with promises of peace and prosperity, the government sent more troops to stop him. Ney promised to bring him back to Paris "in an iron cage". But when his men met Napoleon's at Auxerre, they went over to Napoleon, and their commander followed suit. The local prefect, having just appealed to "every man of good will" to stop the usurper, then urged people to "unite around this hero whom glory has recalled to us". Louis left Paris for Belgium on 19 March, and Napoleon entered the city the following day.

Emmanuel de Grouchy (1766–1847)

Grouchy was an officer before the Revolution but helped put down royalist risings in the Vendée. He commanded a division and a cavalry corps, being wounded 19 times. In the retreat from Moscow he led the all-officer *bataillon sacrée* that guarded Napoleon. Promoted Marshal in 1815, he was given command of the right wing of the Army of the North, and failed to pursue Blücher after Ligny, though Napoleon's orders were far from explicit. The Bourbons did not confirm his marshalcy, which was restored to him by Louis-Philippe.

The powers at Vienna declared "that Napoleon Bonaparte is placed outside civil and social relations, and that as an enemy and disturber of the peace, he has delivered himself open to public prosecution". On 25 March, Austria, Britain, Prussia and Russia agreed to march against him. Wellington turned down an appointment on the allied staff to command a British, German and Dutch-Belgian force assembling in the Low Countries, and the allies began to mobilize at least 800,000 men. Wellington had over 100,000 around Brussels; Blücher would advance from Namur on Liège with 117,000 Prussians; Schwarzenberg's 210,000 Austrians would move up through the Black Forest, and 75,000 more Austrians and Italians would invade the Riviera from Italy. Lastly, 150,000 Russians would trudge up to the Rhine to form a reserve. But this powerful apparatus would not be ready until July, and the Russians might be later still.

Even Napoleon's supporters affirmed that France did not want war, and there was unrest in the provinces, especially in the royalist south-west. Although mobilization was ordered on 12 April, Napoleon avoided conscription for another three weeks. But even with its aid he would be hard pressed to raise more than 500,000 men in all, and concluded that a defensive strategy might only work if he was prepared to manoeuvre as he had in 1814. The alternative was to lunge hard at the nearest enemy armies, in the Low Countries, hoping that early victory might tilt the political and military balance in his favour.

On 15 June, Napoleon moved the *Armée du Nord*, about 122,000 men in two wings and a reserve, straight for the hinge between Wellington and Blücher. Berthier, his trusted chief of staff, had died under suspicious circumstances. He had left the capable Davout in Paris as war minister and appointed Soult, a field commander rather than a staff officer, as chief of staff. Although Wellington and Blücher had discussed what to do in such a contingency, Napoleon surprised them, and on 16 June, beat the Prussians at Ligny (both sides roughly equal at something over 80,000 apiece) on his right, although Ney (with over 20,000 men at the start of the battle, and more arriving in the course of the day) was blocked by Wellington (starting with just 8,000 men, but also being reinforced as the battle went on) the same day at Quatre Bras on his left. Nevertheless, the campaign had opened auspiciously for Napoleon.

CHAPTER THIRTY-TWO

THE IMPERIAL

GUARD

**The Guard formed the core upon which
Napoleon relied.**

In November 1799, the Guards of the Directory and Legislature were reconstituted as the Consular Guard, and in January 1800 its strength was fixed at 2,089 men, infantry, cavalry and artillery, with its horsemen – eventually renamed "Horse Grenadiers" – commanded by Bessières, who was to have a long association with the Guard. Already the Guard had advantages: officers and men enjoyed extra pay, improved allowances and administrative autonomy. The Guard fought well in its first battle at Marengo, and *La Marche de La Garde Consulaire à Marengo* became a classic of French military music.

In 1801 the Commander in Chief's guides joined the Guard, becoming its *Chasseurs à Cheval*, whose green undress uniform was Napoleon's favourite. The Guard grew again in 1802, gaining engineer officers (noncommissioned men appeared in 1810) and its own commissariat. The foot grenadiers (big men) and chasseurs (nimble fellows) were each styled a "corps", so it was clear that Napoleon planned to increase the Guard, making it into an army in miniature. Mameluke horsemen, dressed in Turkish style, were added, with Marines of the Guard appearing in 1803 and Guard gendarmes the following year. In January 1804, Napoleon created the *vélites* of the Guard to encourage middle-class boys into the army, and amongst those who learned their trade with them was Bugeaud, future Marshal of France and conqueror of Algeria.

The Guard became Imperial on 10 May 1804: the pay of its senior officers was increased, and line troops were to present arms when it passed. By 1805, the Guard, 7,000 strong, constituted an all-arms division under Bessières, and its cavalry charged the Russian Guard at Austerlitz, although the infantry were not committed and "cried with rage". A dragoon regiment, the Empress's Dragoons, was added in 1806, with a fusilier regiment, part of the corps of grenadiers, the same year. There was resentment when the Guard was not committed at Jena, though it made a fine triumphal entry into Berlin. The Guard cavalry distinguished itself at Eylau, and the foot grenadiers, husbanded for just such an emergency, threw the Russians out of the cemetery at the close of that dreadful day.

A corps of horsed *Gendarmes d'Ordonnance* was raised to encourage the old regime's aristocrats into the army, but it was not well received and was disbanded in 1807. The Polish Lancers of the Guard, raised that year, charged against impossible odds at Somosierra on the road to Madrid in 1808, and a detachment accompanied Napoleon to Elba in 1814. A second lancer regiment, known as the Red Lancers, was added in 1810 after the annexation of Holland, many of its men coming from the hussars of the Dutch Guard. A third regiment was raised in Lithuania but destroyed in Russia the same year. Three regiments of *Eclaireurs à Cheval* appeared in 1813, but two were speedily transferred to the line and the third, Polish-recruited, sent back to Poland.

The Guard infantry also grew, with the corps of grenadiers including not only the Grenadiers of the Guard, the quintessential bear-skinned *grognards* or "grumblers," (with a Dutch regiment from 1810), but regiments of fusiliers, tirailleurs, conscripts and flankers, some of which endured while others did not. A similar process saw the corps of chasseurs take on new units, enabling the lustre of the Guard to be shared widely across the army. As the Guard expanded into a self-contained corps, it was subdivided to preserve graduations of status. For the 1815 campaign, for instance, it comprised three infantry divisions, the Old, Middle and Young Guard, with heavy and light cavalry and an artillery of 118 guns – over 20,000 men in all.

There is no doubting the Guard's quality. There were battles, like Borodino, when Napoleon refused to hazard it, his last reserve, but when he did commit it, the effect was often decisive. The repulse of the Guard at Waterloo was profoundly significant: as the last of the old grumblers fell back down the trampled slope, it was indeed the end of an empire.

CHAPTER THIRTY-THREE

THE 100 DAYS: WATERLOO

Early on 17 June, Wellington, then at Quatre Bras, heard that Blücher had been beaten at Ligny, but he told the Prussian liaison officer that he would fight on the ridge of Mont St Jean if Blücher would assist him.

In his commander's absence – the old warrior had been unhorsed and ridden over at Ligny – Gneisenau, Blücher's Chief of Staff, had decided to fall back on Liège, concentrating first at Wavre. When Blücher reappeared, he countermanded the order: soldierly honour and common sense urged him to join Wellington. Napoleon made a slow start on 17 June. He expected the Prussians to head for Liège, but was surprised to find Wellington still at Quatre Bras. Late that morning, he told Grouchy to make for Gembloux, keeping in touch with the Prussians. Wellington, meanwhile, broke contact, assisted by a heavy thunderstorm, and the night of 17 June saw him at Mont St Jean with 68,000 men. Napoleon, with 72,000, spent the night in the farmhouse of Le Caillou, and early on 18 June, he met his senior officers there. Soult urged him to order Grouchy back, but the Emperor sent an obscurely worded order telling Grouchy to keep the Prussians – still over 80,000 strong – out of the battle.

Henry William Paget, Earl of Uxbridge and Marquess of Anglesey (1768–1854)

As Lord Paget he raised a foot regiment in 1793, but soon became known as a cavalry theorist. He commanded Moore's cavalry in the Peninsula, but his affair with Wellington's sister-in-law made it impossible for him to serve under Wellington until 1815, when, as Lord Uxbridge, he commanded the cavalry and was effectively the duke's second in command. He lost a leg at Waterloo and was made Marquess immediately afterwards. He was subsequently active in politics, serving both as Master General of the Ordnance and Lord Lieutenant of Ireland.

Napoleon proposed to feint at Hougoumont, the farmhouse complex on Wellington's right centre, and then strike up the main Brussels road bisecting the position. This attack would be supported by 84 12-pounder guns just west of the road and, as the ground was boggy, would be delayed until 1.00 a.m. to give it time to dry out. This was to the allied advantage. At 9.30 a.m. Blücher told Wellington that he would march to join him, and set off at the head of Bülow's corps. Grouchy, lacking clear orders and unused to independent command, failed to interpose himself between the Prussians and Wellington. The battle would be a race against time: could Napoleon beat Wellington before Blücher arrived?

Jerome Bonaparte's division of Reille's corps attacked Hougoumont just before midday, and the fighting sucked in reinforcements from both sides. D'Erlon's attack went in up the main road at about 1.30 a.m., and reached the crest-line, assailed by artillery fire all the way there and checked by musketry at the top. It was broken by Lord Uxbridge's British cavalry, but the horsemen hurtled on into the French gun-line and were cut to pieces. Ney then sent a succession of cavalry charges up the slope, parallel with and west of the main road, to be received by Wellington's infantry in squares, and at about 6.00 a.m. the farm of La Haye Sainte, on the main road, was wrested from its defenders, men of the King's German Legion, by infantry attack. By this time, however, the Prussians were making their presence felt on the French right, and although Napoleon sent the Young Guard up to check them, it was evident that he was running out of time.

William, Prince of Orange (1792–1849)

The son of William I of the Netherlands, William was forced into exile by the French at the age of three. Educated at Berlin and Oxford, in 1811 he became aide-de-camp to Wellington in Spain. In 1815 he commanded one of Wellington's corps, and his mistakes reflected his inexperience. At Quatre Bras he ordered some British battalions to move from square into line, in the face of protests, although there was French cavalry at hand: his troops were immediately charged and badly cut about. At Waterloo he launched Colonel Ompteda's King's German Legion battalion in a hopeless counter-attack against La Haye Sainte. But nobody could doubt his courage, and he himself was wounded. In 1830 he tried unsuccessfully to prevent the split between the Dutch and Belgian portions of his father's kingdom. Reigning as William II from 1830, he was initially conservative, but in 1848 oversaw a new constitution which limited royal power.

The battle was at its climax, and Wellington's army was cruelly battered. At about 7.00 p.m. Napoleon sent grenadiers and chasseurs of his Guard against Wellington's right centre, but, as they reached the crest they were greeted with point-blank musketry, and flanking fire from the 52nd Light Infantry, at right angles to the main line. As the Guard folded back, Wellington ordered a general advance, but his own cavalry were so exhausted that it was Prussian horsemen who pushed on to sabre fugitives under the light of the moon.

CHAPTER THIRTY-FOUR

IMPERIAL

TWILIGHT:

ST HELENA

**There was no immediate military reason
for Waterloo to prove decisive.**

Casualties for the campaign were around 60,000 French to almost 55,000 allied. Soult had reconstituted the *Armée du Nord*, the Austrians had been checked in Piedmont, and Schwarzenberg's advance guard had been beaten. But there was no widespread support for Napoleon. When he reached Paris on 21 June, the Chambers demanded his abdication. He recognized that the game was up, and abdicated in favour of his son on 22 June. A provisional government agreed to an armistice, the Convention of Paris. The eventual peace punished France for the Hundred Days by returning her to the borders of 1789, stripping away the gains of the Revolution.

Napoleon retired to Malmaison and considered his future. He proposed to go to the United States: "They will give me some land, or I shall buy

Hudson Lowe (1769-1844)

Lowe was born in Galway, son of an army surgeon. Commissioned into the 50th Foot in 1787, he raised the Corsican Rangers, composed of anti-French Corsicans, and commanded it in Egypt before holding a series of senior appointments in the Mediterranean. In 1813-14 he was attached to the allied armies and served in their major battles, being selected to bring news of Napoleon's 1814 abdication to London. Knighted and promoted Major-General, he was made Governor of St Helena in 1815. Lowe was firm and tactless rather than gratuitously harsh, but lost the propaganda battle.

some, and we will cultivate it, living on the products of my fields and flocks." However, when he reached Bordeaux and boarded the French frigate *La Saale*, he found that Captain Maitland of HMS *Bellerophon* had been authorized to take him and his entourage on board. He left France for ever on Saturday 15 July. *Bellerophon* took him to Portsmouth, where he was transferred to HMS *Northumberland* on 7 August. Ten weeks later he arrived at the island of St Helena, a volcanic outcrop in the South Atlantic.

Napoleon was accommodated in Longwood House, six kilometres (four miles) from the island's tiny capital, Jamestown. The circumstances of his stay there remain deeply controversial. He was allowed a small entourage – General and Madame Bertrand, Count and Countess Montholon, General Gourgaud, and his secretary, the historian Emmanuel de Las Casas, who would help him with his memoirs. He had servants, silver plate, and a liberal allowance of food and wine, and was permitted to ride within 20km (12 miles) – later 13km (eight miles) – of Longwood. Yet he was unquestionably a prisoner. He was escorted when he left the house, all his correspondence had to pass through the governor's office for censoring, there was a large garrison to prevent attempted rescues, the climate was uncongenial and Longwood was damp.

Major-General Sir Hudson Lowe became Governor of St Helena in April 1816. He was a 46-year-old veteran who spoke French, German and the Corsican dialect of Italian. A recent supporter describes "a dedicated public servant who found himself saddled with the unenviable task of having to enforce the strict, detailed orders given him by London". In contrast, the spleen of his critics was fuelled by correspondence which reflected Napoleon's orders to "make Europe learn how badly we are being treated here, so that they may become indignant". Lowe addressed Napoleon, on orders from London, as "General Bonaparte", and at their final interview told him: "Your misconception of my character and the rudeness of your manners excite my pity.' Lowe dismissed Barry O'Meara, the naval surgeon who attended Napoleon, ostensibly for helping get uncensored letters off the island, but in fact, claim Napoleon's supporters, for kindness towards his patient. The best that we can say is that Lowe was a punctilious jailer but no sadist, and that much of the unhappiness at Longwood came from the claustrophobic atmosphere within Napoleon's entourage.

In 1818, it was clear that Napoleon was ill, and by 1820 his violent stomach aches and fits of vomiting reduced him to a diet of fluids. His doctor, Antommarchi, prescribed camomel, but, after a period of intense suffering, on the morning of 5 May 1821, Napoleon died. An autopsy concluded that he had died of stomach cancer, like his father, but this has been vigorously challenged. Tests on his hair revealed unusually high quantities of arsenic, and the weight of opinion (most recently confirmed by *Le Quotidien du Médicin* on 7 June 2005) now favours death by poisoning, with Montholon, who stood not only to escape from exile, but also to receive a substantial legacy on Napoleon's death, as the most likely culprit.

Charles Tristan, Comte de Montholon (1782–1853)

Montholon maintained that his military career began in 1798 and culminated in promotion to General. However, some recent scholars have discovered no trace of this, though the Bourbons made him Brigadier in 1814. He accompanied Napoleon to St Helena and played a major part in discrediting Lowe. Those subscribing to the theory Napoleon was murdered see Montholon as the probable culprit, either because he was a beneficiary of Napoleon's will, or because he had been suborned by the Bourbons. Imprisoned in 1840 for supporting Louis Napoleon's Boulogne coup, he sat as a deputy in the Second Republic. The case against him is strong but unprovable.

N A P O L E O N ' S

L E G A C Y

Napoleon was buried – with military honours furnished by 2,000 men of the garrison of St Helena – in his favourite uniform of the *Chasseurs à Cheval* of the Guard. But he would not rest there.

The Bourbons, brought back "in the baggage train of the allies", set about a purge of prefects and other officials, and the "White Terror" saw the execution or murder of several thousand Bonapartists, often lynched to settle local scores. But as memories of the wars faded, neither the restored Bourbons nor the Orleanist July monarchy, which ruled from 1830 to 1848, could offer sufficient lustre to outshine a distant gleam of eagles. A man born in 1815 remembered: "When the Emperor was talked about, it wasn't to deplore his appalling human butcheries, but to remind we little ones that his eyes were not cold and for 20 years he gave our enemies rude shocks." The moderate republicanism that

Carl Maria Gottleib von Clausewitz (1780–1831)

Clausewitz joined the Prussian army in 1792 and fought at Jena in 1806. He resigned his commission and served in the Russian army in 1812–14, and, restored to the Prussian service, was a corps chief of staff at Waterloo. Although he died without exercising operational command, Clausewitz became a thinker of enduring importance. His seminal book *On War*, published posthumously by his wife in 1832, has influenced military thinking for generations and is still in print today. He admired Napoleon's readiness for "risking everything in decisive battles", and his work, with its emphasis on battle, the political character of war, and the "friction" that distinguished real war from theory, reflected his own experience of the Napoleonic wars.

characterized much opposition to Bourbons and Orleanists was mingled with a new, supple political force: Bonapartism.

The Emperor's memory was kept fresh. Half-pay officers muttered in cafés, and impoverished veterans flicked back the lapel of a threadbare greatcoat to show their Legion of Honour and earn a salute from a sentry. Cheap coloured prints showed Napoleon on a dozen stricken fields; drawings of the violet, with which he was particularly associated, embodied concealed images of Napoleon, Marie-Louise and their son the King of Rome; his birthday, 15 August, was reverently celebrated. Balzac conjured up the character Gondrin, who had been a sapper on the Berezina and hailed his emperor from its freezing waters, and Hugo wrote of the "dismal plain" of Waterloo, blaming the weather ("a drop of water, nothing more") for depriving his hero of victory. When Napoleon's body was brought back to France in 1840 for re-interment in Les Invalides, the Napoleonic legacy had been reinvented. "Above all," declaimed a popular newspaper, "it was revolutionary France, represented at this ceremony by the veterans of the armies of the Republic and Empire, that the people of Paris came to salute, touched by all these memories of our glorious past."

His nephew, Louis Napoleon, capitalized on this sentiment to win election as president of the Second Republic in December 1848, and to secure power by staging his own Brumaire in December 1851. He became Emperor a year later, styling himself Napoleon III (for although the King

Napoleon III, Emperor of the French (1808–1873)

Napoleon III was the third son of Louis Bonaparte. On the death of Napoleon's son in 1832, he became head of the dynasty, mounting unsuccessful coups in 1836 and 1840. In 1848 he was elected to the Constituent Assembly, and was swiftly voted President. Seizing sole power in 1851, he was proclaimed Emperor a year later. His reign brought material prosperity and left a lasting mark on Paris, but his military adventures culminated in the Franco-Prussian war. He was captured at Sedan in 1870, and lived in England until his death. His only son was killed in the 1879 Anglo-Zulu War.

of Rome never reigned, but died in 1832, with his Austrian title the Duke of Reichstadt, he would have been Napoleon II), and ruled until his capture at Sedan in 1870 during the Franco-Prussian war. Bonapartism was still not a spent force, but the death of Napoleon III's only son the Prince Imperial, killed in action during the Zulu War of 1879, was a setback from which it never recovered.

Yet if Bonapartism was broken by the end of the nineteenth century, Napoleon's legacy lived well beyond it. The *Code Napoléon* still forms the basis of French civil law, and finds answering echoes in the legal codes of some of the countries which became French allies. France's administrative and education system would still make sense to the Emperor. It is tempting for some Frenchmen to compare the European Union with Napoleon's empire, and to see him as the first great European, demolishing political and commercial barriers and, but for British intransigence, establishing a unified continent. If he lost Waterloo in 1815, he has won it since. The cafés and souvenir shops that cluster in the centre of the allied position have more bronzes, commemorative plates and assorted knick-knacks of Napoleon, who was defeated, than they do of Wellington or Blücher, who were victorious. And that, perhaps, is a symbol of his enduring appeal. We too easily forget his overweening egotism and his shocking cynicism, his destructive wars and vain conquests, and remember instead the man on horseback who rose from nothing and who made Frenchmen, almost despite themselves, masters of a continent.

I N D E X

Page numbers in **bold** refer to main entries; page numbers in *italics* refer to illustrations/photographs/captions

Hertfordshire Libraries

Croxley Green Library
Kiosk 1

Customer ID: *****8744

Items that you have renewed

Title: The Napoleonic Wars
Due: 23 December 2020

Total items: 1
Account balance: £0.00
02/12/2020 11.35
Checked out: 1
Overdue: 0
Reservations: 0
Ready for collection: 0

Thank you for using Hertfordshire
Libraries
Enquiries / Renewals go to:
www.hertfordshire.gov.uk/libraries
or call: 0300 123 4049

Hertfordshire
Libraries

ACKNOWLEDGEMENTS

The publishers would like to dedicate this book to Gwladys Longeard, whose help and enthusiasm have been invaluable.

Thanks are also extended to the following for additional assistance with the preparation of the first edition of this book:
Sonia Land
Steph Muir
Photothèque du musée de l'Armée / Agence photographique de la RMN, 10 rue de l'Abbaye, 75006 Paris, France
Laurent Bergeot
The National Archives, Kew, Richmond, Surrey, TW9 4DU
Paul Johnson
The National Army Museum, Royal Hospital Road, Chelsea, London SW3 4HT
Dr A. Massie and Joanna Quill
Service historique de la Défense, Château de Vincennes, BP 107, 00481 Armées, Paris, France
Gwladys Longeard, Alain Morgat and Claude Ponnou

PICTURES AND PHOTOGRAPHS